The Rules of the Money Making Game

Dr. Mariyan Genchev

Copyright © 2019 Dr. Mariyan Genchev

All rights reserved.

ISBN-13: 9781796688528

DEDICATION

This book is dedicated to everyone that think that making money is hard. Managing money is a game and as long as you know the rules you have an advantage while playing it that will help you win. Money – it can be an enemy, that you have to fight or a friend indeed for your whole life.

CONTENTS

Acknowledgments	i
INTRODUCTION	1
PART I: THE PSYCHOLOGICAL RULES OF THE MONEY MAKING GAME	24
Mindsets of the rich and the poor	25
Change management	80
Time management	113
Turning motivation into habit	146
PART II: THE PRACTICAL RULES OF THE MONEY MAKING GAME	163
Basic money principles	164
Making the first budget	194
Debt free	232
Making our money work for us	251
Conclusion	271
About the author	274
Further readings	275

ACKNOWLEDGMENTS

I want to start by thanking my awesome friend Dr. Mladen Lambeff for all the financial advices and work that he did on this book. Thank you so much, without you this book might have never been completed.

I also want to thank to my family - my amazing wife and my two daughters for all their support.
Last but not least, my friends that have enough time and patience to give me both positive and negative feedback.

INTRODUCTION

"If you must play, decide on three things at the start: the rules of the game, the stakes, and the quitting time."

Chinese proverb

Money making is easy, it is just like a game, and as such it can be mastered, regardless how difficult it might look at first. Of course, we have to learn the rules before we start playing. Practicing the game and playing by the rules will eventually make us good at it – that is all we will need in order to win. But this comes up with a price – we should work really hard and believe in ourselves to achieve that.

For some people becoming rich may seem impossible, while others may find it easy and fun. The truth is that it, as everything else, can be learned and believe us, it is not a rocket science.

There are two main aspects that we must keep under consideration when we talk about transitioning from the poor and middle class to the 3% of the people that are rich. These aspects can be generally described as:
- Psychological aspect of money making;
- Practical aspect of money making.

1. Psychological aspect of money making

"All money is a matter of belief."

Adam Smith

From psychological point of view, the main reason why we are not rich at the moment, is most probably the fact that we are not resourceful enough. This means that we should build a solid base of knowledge that will help us with our journey to success. This book will try to provide us with the basic steps on how to start building our wealth and become financially independent.

So what are the main psychological limitations that are holding us back from becoming rich? Below we have listed some of the most common reasons leading to these limitations:
- We use excuses;
- We don't take enough responsibility;
- We have too many limiting beliefs;
- We have too much social conditioning;
- We are prohibited from becoming successful, because of our way of thinking;
- We are afraid of change.

We use excuses

"I respect my limitations, but I don't use them as an excuse."

Stephen R. Donaldson

Every time we fail to accomplish some task, target, project, or even a dream in our life, we tend to blame someone or something for the way things have turned out. One of the common skills of rich people is that they do not hide behind excuses. They use every failure as an experience, and never make the same mistake twice. Poor people, on the other hand, act quite differently. They love to accuse others for their own lack of success. Moreover, they are convinced that whatever happens – it is simply not their fault, which gives them a false sense of security.

We don't take enough responsibility

> *"Whatever happens, take responsibility."*
>
> ***Tony Robbins***

As much as they like to use excuses, poor people hate to take responsibility. There is always someone else responsible for the things that happen around them. They never hold themselves accountable for their own actions.
The result of such behavior is that it prevents us from growing and evolving.

We have too many limiting beliefs

> *"Remember, we see the world not as it is but as we are. Most of us see through the eyes of our fears and our limiting beliefs and our false assumptions."*
>
> ***Robin S. Sharma***

More or less, our behavior depends on our environment. Certainly, our way of thinking, our actions and our beliefs are influenced to a large extent by our family, friends, school, university, religion, etc. All these factors may lead us to the misconception that we cannot accomplish our dreams and goals. In fact, we all have the potential to create great things and the sooner we understand that, the better.

We have too much social conditioning

"Some habits of ineffectiveness are rooted in our social conditioning toward quick-fix, short-term thinking."

Stephen Covey

This is related to the people with whom we spend most of our time. It is a well-known fact that our performance is based on the average performance of the five people closest to us. So if the ones around us are poor, most probably we will be poor too. In contrast, if we carefully select the people to surround ourselves with, it is more likely that we will move forward at a faster pace.

We are prohibited from becoming successful, because of our way of thinking

"Success is a state of mind. If you want success, start thinking of ourselves as a success."

Joyce Brothers

With time we all develop a certain way of thinking and in most of the cases, based on our friends, relatives, social contacts and media – the way we think is based on the idea that we cannot be or do not need to be rich. The good news here is that negative thoughts can be replaced by a winning mentality, as soon as we realize that they stand in the way of our goals. A good step in that direction is to try and visualize the desired result of our efforts. By doing so we increase our motivation and become even more determined to get it.

We are afraid of change

"I tell all my younger friends: "Don't be afraid of change. That is when you truly see what your destiny is."

Iman

The last item in this list is the ability to change. The truth is that we cannot get new results, if we do the same things over and over again. If we need to move forward with our life, we must understand the basic principles and the emotions we are going through during the change process.

As already stated, in order to become rich the first thing to do is stop using as an excuse any of the following:

- Low current income;
- Local economy;
- Limitations from the country we live in;
- Bad childhood;
- Lack of education;
- Lack of luck;
- Lack of social connections;
- Lack of social status.

Low current income

"I've been around low-income people all of my life. I mean, growing up, low income, the community where I've chosen to live, low-income."

Danny K. Davis

How many times have we heard someone telling us that they cannot get something they want, or that they could not follow their dreams because of their current income? Well this excuse cannot be taken seriously. As a matter of fact, many people are not able to correctly evaluate their financial situation and, most importantly, prefer to stay in their comfort zone instead of facing and overcoming this problem.

Local economy

> *"The poor don't live in functional market economies as the rest of us do, but in political economies where corruption and broken systems extend from local government to moneylenders."*
>
> *Jacqueline Novogratz*

This is one of the main excuses we tend to use to lie to ourselves when we do not want to change our way of living. External factors are certainly important but they are no reason for us to sit and complain. Moreover, economy has its ups and down, meaning that, as time goes on, the business conditions (whatever they are right now) will not remain the same. So if we are truly interested in the economic development of our country, region or city, instead of blaming it for our misfortune, we could analyze the economic data and find new money making opportunities.

Limitations from the country we are currently living in

> *"Heaven is a state of mind, not a location, since Spirit is everywhere and in everything."*
>
> **Wayne Dyer**

This usually comes with the story of all the successful friends and relatives that went to another country and made a lot of money, just because they are abroad. Although there are some exceptions in certain parts of the world, honestly speaking, emigration is not the reason why these people succeed. Their success comes from the fact that they decide to change, take the risk and by going to another country they are forced to get out of their comfort zone and to work as hard as possible. In most of the cases we can get the same or even better results, if we put the same amount of effort in the country we live in.

Bad childhood

"If you carry your childhood with you, you never become older."

Tom Stoppard

As already stated, the environment that we grew up with is one of the main factors for shaping our behavior, but this does not mean that we cannot change it. In principle, every single one of us is different from the rest and our family environment is no exception to that rule. Some have a flying start in their life, while others start with a great load to carry on their backs. However, what really matters is not how we start the race, but where we are going to be when it ends. There are multiple examples of people who have managed to become rich despite their bad childhood.

Lack of education

"In spite of my lack of education, I didn't lack direction."

Chris Cornell

Although education is really important and continuous learning throughout our life is essential, the lack of it should not be used as an excuse. If we find out that we don't have the knowledge and skills needed for our career development, it is never too late to fix that. We should understand that by doing so we make the best investment - invest in ourselves. Nowadays, information of all sorts is more accessible than ever and therefore it is much easier for us to self-improve and lead our life in the direction we want to go. Both online and offline we can find the answers we need - we just have to be curious enough to ask the right questions.

Lack of luck

> *"Luck is great, but most of life is hard work."*
>
> ***Iain Duncan Smith***

Getting rich and wealthy has nothing to do with luck. We must realize that being lucky is a one-off event, while building a fortune is a long-term process. Without having a proper strategy, our luck will help little in improving our personal finances. Let us repeat once more:

playing the money making game is not gambling. It is goal setting, decision making and high motivation.

It makes no sense to sit around and blame our bad luck for the way things are. Instead, we should learn how to work smart and use our time efficiently and effectively. In order to succeed, we have to treasure it as our most precious asset and avoid activities that could waste it.

Lack of social connections

"Social connection is such a basic feature of human experience that when we are deprived of it, we suffer."

Leonard Mlodinow

Our social connections are among the main sources of personal power and influence that can and will significantly speed up our wealth building. As important as it is to have the right contacts, not having them it is not a reason to complain. The simple solution is to start building our network, using all the communication channels available – meetings, seminars, social media, etc. While doing it, we should select carefully the people we surround ourselves with, because it is likely that they will influence our future decisions. In other words, we should go for quality, not quantity.

Lack of social status

> *"Our own relentless search for novelty and social status locks us into an iron cage of consumerism. Affluence has itself betrayed us."*
>
> *Tim Jackson*

Similarly to the social connections, our status is also a major success factor. However people use it quite often as an excuse - lying to themselves that they are not capable to succeed because of their social status. But the fact is that social status is something that we build throughout our whole life. This is not something that most of us are born with and should not be something that stops us from reaching our goals.

All of the above are symptoms of us making ourselves a victim. We need to understand that we cannot be a victim and a millionaire at the same time. Now is the time for us to choose –

do we want to remain a victim or we want to change and do something better with our life.

> ***"We must take sides. Neutrality helps the oppressor, never the victim. Silence encourages the tormentor, never the tormented."***
>
> ***Elie Wiesel***

But if we want to change ourselves and be happier and successful, this book is the beginning of our journey.

The first step is to start taking responsibility for everything we do in our life. Rich people are bosses of their inner selves; they control their emotions and mind.

In our journey of becoming rich there are three main aspects we need to concentrate on:
- Money;
- Career;
- Business.

Of course, these are the three main things that we need to focus on but there are many more things that we must take under consideration and work on as well. We should start getting responsible for our:
- Negative thoughts;
- Neurotic behavior;
- Angry behavior.

In other words, we really have to work hard on improving ourselves. Working on our mindset is essential.

It is important to understand right at the beginning that there are no shortcuts, no cheats and becoming rich has nothing to do with one's luck. If we think that with luck we can become rich, guess what – we won't. We will never get rich this way. If we, in a miraculous way, become rich by winning the lottery for example, we will lose this money very fast, as we won't be able to manage it. This is mostly because we won't have developed the proper mindset to know the true value of money.

To become rich and earn millions we need to start doing radical things with our life. Most people fail to do so because their way of thinking cannot permit them to do so. It was some 250 years ago when one of the American Founding Fathers – **Thomas Jefferson**, stated:

"If you want something you've never had, you must be willing to do something you've never done."

To play the money making game, it is essential to be able to evaluate where we come from. If we come from the middle class or from a poor environment, where every day we are told that there is no way for us to become rich, we will have to eliminate that destructive influence once and for all.

To be honest, rich people do almost the same amount of work as poor people, but they do it in a completely different way. Rich people's mindset and practices are what differentiates them from the poor.

Let's say that we work 40 hours per week from 9 till 5 and we earn somewhere between 50 and 100 thousand dollars per year. How realistic it is to believe that we could have so many pay raises in our life that will make us earn 10-20 times more than what we are currently getting paid? Statistically, the chance is less than 0.1% to get to a top manager position or CEO in our lifetime at our work. That is why we need to develop a radically different way of thinking.

We will also need to find a purpose for generating our wealth. We need to find a greater motivation for ourselves than just earning money. Money alone can never keep us going all the way to our final goal. If we simply want to make money and nothing else, we will lose momentum very fast, as it could not motivate us long enough to reach our destination. Therefore, we will need to think of a valid reason to transition from poor to rich.

For example, most of the successful entrepreneurs want to change or influence the world with their knowledge, experience and effort.

So, to sum it up, in order to accomplish our dreams we should work a lot on our inner self and on developing the right mindset.

2. Practical aspect of money making

"Most social problems could be helped or prevented if people had more money and practical advice."

Sue Townsend

From the practical point of view, the bigger value we provide and the more people we help, the more money we will generate. When speaking about the practical aspect of money making, we must evaluate how we feel and where we are in our journey. We need to ask ourselves the following:

- Is our current job the one that we want to do in five years' time?
- Does it match our education, skills, experience and talent?
- Do we feel underpaid or undervalued?

- Does it let us develop as professionals and do we learn new things every day?
- Does our job allow us to have enough free time?
- Is our job stressing us out?

Is our current job the one that we want to do in five years' time?

"The worst question is, 'Where do you see yourself in five years?' I don't know. Variety is the spice of life. That's the best way to describe it."

Anton du Beke

Let us sit down and think about it – do we see ourselves in the same company and in the same position five years from now? Is this the job that makes us happy? Do we get paid enough to accomplish our long-term goals? If we do not feel this is the job we want to see ourselves doing in five years' time, we should think what can be changed. For instance, if we need a pay rise, we might have to do something extra to get it – some sort of training, certification or simply use our time more effectively, so that we can take on new responsibilities.

Of course, this is not always the case, when we evaluate our situation. Sometimes we need to move away completely from our current job to a different position or even a different industry. Either way, we have to set a strategy to accomplish our goal and start following it.

Does it match our education, skills, experience and talent?

"Follow your dreams and use your natural-born talents and skills to make this a better world for tomorrow."

Paul Watson

The next thing that we need to honestly evaluate is whether we are getting the best out of all our competences and skills. Can we accomplish more, if we use our maximum potential? Most likely we will answer positively to that question. Next, we must ask ourselves whether, with the skills we have, we could do things better or in a different way, so that we can be more successful. Almost every time when we evaluate ourselves, we reach to the conclusion that we can be much more productive, that we can work at a higher position, or that we can start our own business.

Anyway, we shouldn't rush into quick decisions, such as immediately leaving our job to start a business, because without careful planning and proper market research, we can end up being in a worse situation than we are currently in.

Do we feel underpaid or undervalued?

> *"I've kept to myself, I've put my head down. I've gone to work. And I have felt undervalued."*
>
> *Carli Lloyd*

When we speak about work, we all know that we should feel happy doing it. What usually demotivates us and makes us not willing to use our full potential, is being underpaid or undervalued by our managers. If any of these factors exists in our daily job, we need to think how we can change it. Life is too short to do something that we don't like and that makes us feel miserable eight hours a day, five days a week. We work about 40 years throughout our life – who wants to feel undervalued for such a long period of time?

Does it let us develop as professionals and do we learn new things every day?

"Every day, I want to learn something new; I want to move up."

Dinesh Paliwal

As far as motivation is concerned, one of the main factors to choose one job over another is whether it helps us develop as professionals. This is closely related to both improving our qualifications and getting promoted (i.e. better-paid) in the future. Unfortunately, it is very rare that someone has got their dream job allowing them to self-develop as they want to. If that is not our case, it is yet another reason for us to be dissatisfied with what we currently do.

Does our job allow us to have enough free time?

"I regret those times when I've chosen the dark side. I've wasted enough time not being happy."

Jessica Lange

We already discussed that time is our biggest resource. But it is not just the job that is important. We should evaluate whether we have the time to enjoy a balanced life - the so called "work-life balance" is very important for our happiness. Let's think whether our current job can provide us with enough time to enjoy the other things that matter to us. If we are constantly working overtime and, for example, do not have enough time for our family, friends, etc., then we have to consider what we need to change. For most people, this is usually a time-management issue, rather than an issue with the job they have.

Is our job stressing us out?

"People really do think they have to choose between high stress and high reward jobs, and low stress and low reward jobs."

Tim Ferriss

Stress is a very common issue and it prevents us from performing to the best of our abilities, but there is also a side effect that we do not consider. When speaking about the work we do, stress usually comes to show whether we like it or not. Human beings can take a lot of stress when they are doing something they love and cannot handle even small amount of stress when they are doing something that they do not like. It is amazing how much stress we can take. If someone told us that we need to work 24 hours a day without regulated breaks, helping our clients all the time, sometimes even without having the time to sleep, we will probably think this is crazy and that it is not possible. But if we add love to the equation, we will see that most of the mothers in the world do this for their newborn child and they can handle it. The same goes for the doctors doing operations that last over 24 hours.

Again, stress is not an issue with our job, but it is a good indicator if we like it or not.

While going through all the questions on this list, it is very likely that our answers will not be in favor of our current job and maintaining the status quo won't be our long-term goal.

To recap, the whole process of money making boils down to making a critical and honest self-assessment, taking responsibility and acting accordingly. If we have to change something, we will just need to do it and move forward.

PART I:
THE PSYCHOLOGICAL RULES OF THE MONEY MAKING GAME

MINDSETS OF THE RICH AND THE POOR

"Before you can become a millionaire, you must learn to think like one. You must learn how to motivate ourselves to counter fear with courage."

Thomas J. Stanley

In this chapter we are going to review the things that rich people do differently compared to the poor ones. Not that the poor people cannot do these things as well, they simply lack the awareness or the willingness to do them.
The pieces of advice suggested in this book do not guarantee that we will wake up a

millionaire the day after we read it, but they will definitely improve our knowledge about handling money the right way.

1. Things poor people do differently than the rich

> *"The real tragedy of the poor is the poverty of their aspirations."*
>
> *Adam Smith*

Let's start by giving several examples with the most common things showing how poor and rich people differ in handling their finances. Here are some examples what poor people tend to do:
- Do not invest;
- Work for money;
- Prefer to take less now, than wait a while for a better deal;
- Prefer to buy new fancy things that will lose their value fast;
- Do not have a budget;
- Do not have an emergency fund;
- Have a negative mindset;
- Think "OR" and do not look for opportunities to do "AND";
- Think that they know it all;

- Want to look rich in front of everyone;
- Think that to be rich means to be evil;
- Think that the only way to become rich is to get lucky;
- Think working hard, by itself, will eventually get them rich;
- Do not understand the basics of growth;
- Get bad advice and are willing to follow it blindly;
- Spend their money before they get it;
- Rely only on other people to help them reach the top;
- Blame all others for their misfortune;
- Do not believe they are responsible for their own fate and do not look at every failure as a lesson learned;
- Watch TV a lot and/or are into sports;
- Do not care about their health;
- Live in the past;
- Do not use their strengths;
- Do not treat money as a tool, but rather as a goal;
- Do not work towards making the world a better place, as they don't care about it.

Poor people do not invest

"Never stop investing. Never stop improving. Never stop doing something new."

Bob Parsons

Here are two main case scenarios that we observe among poor people when we speak about investment:
- They do not have any savings and they live from paycheck to paycheck – this is something that ⅔ of people do.
- They have savings but do not invest this money in anything – this is something that the middle class people usually do.

In contrast, rich people always save money and invest in every good opportunity that arises. In other words, not only do they have savings in their bank accounts, but they also invest and try to make the money work for them. **Dan Gertler**, a billionaire businessman, has come up with the following observation:

"Everyone comes with dreams and illusions and promises. Everyone wants quick deals. They don't want to invest."

Poor people work for money

"I'm not rich enough to buy cheap things!"

British proverb

Don't get us wrong here - everybody works for money. However, this is just the first step and if we limit ourselves to it, we risk being poor in the long run. So what are the next steps? Follow the example of rich people who always try to make money work for them. In other words, it is not important how much we get paid per hour, week, month or year. The important thing is to multiply the money earned.

Along these lines, when it comes to spending, we should aim to get the best value for our money. Rich people buy for lifetime – This is based on the idea that it is better to spend twice as much on something that we will use five years, instead of buying it at half price, only to change it after one year of usage.

Poor people prefer to take less now, than wait a while for a better deal

"The key to everything is patience. You get the chicken by hatching the egg, not by smashing it."

Arnold H. Glasow

This is based on human psychology. Most of the people prefer to have 5 dollars now instead of having 15 dollars after a week. They might call their decision "playing safe" but more often than not it simply shows lack of patience to wait for a better option to arrive. Certainly, we are not talking about excessive risk taking or gambling, but rather about comparing various alternatives and picking up the most profitable one.

On the other hand, rich people prefer to go for the best deal even if it takes some time to strike it. They can control their emotions in critical moments and know that to win the money making game one needs perfect planning and perseverance.

Poor people prefer to buy new fancy things that will lose their value fast

> *"The best way to make a good deal is to have the ability to walk away from it."*
>
> *Brian Koslow*

We have to stop wasting money to impress others and focus on what we really need. There is a huge difference between looking rich and being rich. Quite often poor people tend to overspend on fancy stuff they cannot afford. The consequences? Getting into debt and becoming even poorer.

In contrast, even though they have enough money, some rich people could opt to buy a second-hand car in a good condition instead of a brand new car, as they know that it will lose much of its value in the first year. Using a quality car for ten years allows them to get the full value of their purchase.

Poor people do not have a budget

Rich people control their spending – there is a Scottish saying stating:

> *"A penny saved is a penny earned"*

Every state, company, bank, NGO, etc. takes financial planning very seriously and creates its own budget. This is how they control their incoming and outgoing money flows and work towards profit maximization, long-term development and sustainability. In other words, this is how they manage and optimize their finances.

Poor people, for their part, do not have budget plans and spend as much as they earn. Thus, if they have a pay rise, they will automatically rise their spending. They can always find something more expensive to buy, but that is not likely to improve much their quality of life.

On the other hand, having a budget will help us put the additional income into good use – to save and invest more. As we mentioned before, finding different ways to multiply our money is crucial and leads to long-term positive effects. In short, extra money means more opportunities to the rich and higher consumption to the poor.

Poor people do not have an emergency fund

"I get so frustrated when people tell me it's unrealistic to create an eight-month emergency savings fund, or have

money saved for a home down payment, or pay off their $5,000 credit card balance."

Suze Orman

One of the red lines between the poor and the rich is the fact that if the former lose their main source of income they couldn't maintain a normal living standard for more than 3 months. In contrast, rich people have an emergency fund that can easily cover their expenses for a longer period of time. The side effect being that when poor people lose their job they have no other choice but to get the first job available. Rich people, on the other hand, can choose from a lot more options and accept the one that they will make the most of.

As we play the money making game, things cannot go our way all the time. However, being prepared to face the setbacks will greatly reduce their impact on us and will allow us to overcome them quickly. Therefore, if we realize the benefit of having an emergency fund, we lay the groundwork of our financial strategy to become rich.

Poor people have a negative mindset

In general, while rich people have a positive mindset, poor people tend to complain all the time and surround themselves with other negative people. On the contrary, rich people prefer to communicate and interact with other successful and optimistic people. It is a well-known fact that positive environment improves productivity by 30%. Let us refer to the famous remark by ***Henry Ford***:

> ***"Whether you think you can, or you think you cannot – you're right."***

These wise words support the thesis that in order to achieve great results, we have to care about the things we do and to believe in ourselves. There will always be problems along the way, but we should not be discouraged by them, keeping our eyes on the goal.

Poor think "OR" and do not look for opportunities to do "AND"

> ***"Choice is a form of compromise, no? So why choose if you can have both?"***
>
> ***Neri Oxman***

This means that if we have the option to buy one of two things, poor people will struggle and will be forced to choose only one of the options, giving up the other one. On the other hand, rich people will try to get the most of any situation and will look for opportunities to have them both at the same time.

Let's say that we have enough money to get an ice cream or a chocolate bar. Poor people will simply choose one of these options. What rich people will do is try to double their money, so that they can afford both the ice cream and the chocolate bar.

Similar examples could be given with two investment alternatives put on the table, or with two promising ideas for future business endeavors.

Poor people think that they know it all

"Wisdom is the right use of knowledge. To know is not to be wise. Many men know a great deal, and are all the greater fools for it. There is no fool so great a fool as a knowing fool. But to know how to use knowledge is to have wisdom."

Charles Spurgeon

Poor people stop educating and developing themselves at some point in their life. They have no motivation to reach new heights in their profession or field of expertise and are convinced that they know all about it. This is a huge mistake because every day offers a great number of opportunities for learning new things and putting them into practice. Rich people behave in the opposite way – they are aware that the world is changing and they constantly try to acquire new skills and competences. They read a lot and self-improve all the time because they are convinced, and rightly so, that knowledge is power.

Poor people want to look rich in front of everyone

"Too many people spend money they earned...to buy things they don't want...to impress people that they don't like."

Will Rogers

For poor people it is crucial to impress everyone, to have feedback and validation. For instance, they find the brand of their clothes more important than the quality of the fabrics or the comfort to wear them. Poor people also like to come up with a fancy job position in order to impress the ones around them. Also, they love to demonstrate a standard of living that they cannot afford. A textbook example for that is poor people buying on credit expensive new cars, latest shiny phones and gadgets.

On the other hand, rich people do not feel like showing off, they do not need to impress people as they have a realistic estimation of their own abilities. Rich people prefer to focus not so much on looking rich, but rather on their well-being and happiness. They are eager to be respected for their personal qualities and individuality.

Poor people think that to be rich means to be evil

> ***"Money doesn't change men, it merely unmasks them."***
>
> ***Henry Ford***

Although society and some religions try to make us think this way, the truth is different. Certainly, the fastest way to get rich is by being involved in criminal activity, but in general the rich have become rich by following their passion, taking advantage of every opportunity and using their strengths to reach their goals. Therefore, it is not right to equate being rich to being evil.

Also, a rich person is in a much better position to do good for others, than a poor one. Apart from providing jobs for many people, he or she can sponsor young talents, donate money for noble causes, finance new inventions, etc.

Poor people think that luck is the only way to become rich

> *"I'm a great believer in luck, and I find the harder I work the more I have of it."*
> *Thomas Jefferson*

This is the reason why the vast majority of lottery-ticket buyers are poor. Hope without action won't get us rich. Instead of hoping to become wealthy, we need to change our mindset and make it happen, or as the Chinese wisdom quote teaches:

> *"Do what one says."*

The sooner we understand this notion, the better. Instead of starting from the end, we must start from the beginning and be realistic about it - it takes time and effort to win the money making game. We should give more and we will certainly get more. Eventually, the win will be so much sweeter, knowing that it is well deserved.

Poor people think that only working hard will get them rich

> *"I don't believe in luck or in hard work without the so called "work smart". It's not all about how you work hard but it's about how you manage your time, resources, mind to work together for a better output."*
>
> *Jayson Zabate*

In reality, although it is essential that we give our best at work, it is better to work smart than hard. Having said that, these two ways of working are not in conflict. The point is that hard work alone might not be enough for us to achieve our goals. From time to time we need to take a step back and look outside of the box.

We have to figure out whether putting our efforts into what we currently do will get us where we want to be, or some change would be required. The risk that we try to avoid here is to put all our energy into a job that is not worth it and, by doing so, to miss far better money making opportunities.

Poor people do not understand the basics of growth

> *"Success is the sum of small positive actions repeated daily for extended periods of time".*
>
> ***Robert Collier***

The truth is that if there were a fast and easy way of becoming rich, everyone would do it. Success is not something that we wake up with one morning - and there it is. Not at all! It is a long journey during which we must learn how to adapt quickly to different challenges and multiply our money day by day. Becoming more and more experienced, we will be able to eliminate certain mistakes that we make and speed up our trip.

As we already mentioned, poor people look only for the end result. Rich people, for their part, concentrate on the process of becoming wealthy. That is why poor people are not very good at talking about money. Even if they look rich, we can easily spot them by asking some basic questions about building a fortune. They just cannot hold up a deeper conversation about real wealth.

Poor people get bad advice and are willing to follow it blindly

> *"Don't let anyone rent a space in your head, unless they're a good tenant."*
>
> *Unknown author*

Poor people cannot differentiate a good piece of advice from a bad one. They ask for advice the people around them no matter what their particular knowledge or field of expertise is. As a result, instead of a professional opinion they get a mix of suggestions, beliefs and emotions that are not based on facts. Such an advice, even though it may be given with good intentions, is highly unlikely to lead to a correct decision. This approach is definitely wrong and we must do our best to avoid it.

Rich people prefer to get advice from someone that inspires them – a top expert, a role model, a well-known specialist, etc. They value other people's talent and achievements and know how hard it is for somebody to become an authority in their field.

Poor people spend their money before they get it

> *"Never spend your money before you have it."*
>
> ***Thomas Jefferson***

They use credit cards to buy things. The worst part is that poor people spend their money in advance on something that they do not need or do it only to impress someone. These days it is very easy to get what we want here and now. But it comes with a price to pay. Financial institutions love this part of human behavior as it makes their million-dollar profits. Every credit card or loan comes with an interest rate. We can think that it is worth it paying back an extra 5% later to have something at the moment. Well, think again. If the bank makes a profit, then we are the ones paying for it. Rich people, on the other hand, prefer to get what they need, once they have enough money to pay for it. It is almost impossible to see them taking consumer loans. If a rich man borrows money, it would most likely be an investment loan. To do it, he or she has already made a business plan with a pretty simple final goal: to make more money than the amount borrowed for the same period of time.

Poor people wait for others to help them reach the top

> *"Don't let others tell you what you cannot do. Don't let the limitations of others limit your vision. If you can remove your self-doubt and believe in ourselves, you can achieve what you never thought possible."*
>
> ***Roy T. Bennett***

Poor people always wait for something extraordinary to happen and for someone to pull them to the top and never follow through on their ideas and potential. This is so disappointing - we only have one life to live and if we don't try to get the best of it but load it with false expectations, there is no chance for us to be happy and successful.

Rich people believe in themselves and look for opportunities that can be used to reach the top. Planning is an important part of their life strategy - they know where they want to be in 1, 5 or even 10 years from now. They are the ones who take the decisions and are responsible for the consequences of these decisions. Needless to say, rich people do not wait for anyone to create their own happiness.

Poor people blame all others for their misfortune

"When you keep blaming others for every mistake you make in life one day you'll look back and realize you're the mistake all along."

Abdulazeez Henry Musa

This is the negative side of the problem that we have just discussed - as they fail to find anybody to win the game for them, poor people make a drama out of it. Being irresponsible is one of their most common characteristics and they always find someone to blame for their failure.

Poor people always have an excuse why their last project failed – because of something not related to their actions. It is true that there are circumstances beyond our control but those should never be used as an excuse. Shifting responsibility onto others is even worse.

Let us refer to another quote on the subject which belongs to **John Burroughs**:

"You can get discouraged many times, but you are not a failure until you begin to blame somebody else and stop trying."

When they are faced with a serious problem, the last thing rich people would do is blame someone else for it. They would analyze their actions in detail, trying to find out what could be done better and would aim to solve the problem as soon as possible.

Poor people do not believe they are responsible for their own fate and do not look at every failure as a lesson learned

"I have not failed. I've just found 10,000 ways that won't work."

Thomas A. Edison

We know that it sounds more like some form of a superstition than reasonable thinking, but poor people tend to believe nothing is in their control and the story of their life had been written before they were even born. They find it self-comforting to explain their failures with the phrase: "It was meant to be like this" instead of trying to learn from their mistakes and not repeat them in the future.

In contrast, the rich do not include any supernatural forces in the equation. They think of every problem that occurs as a new challenge to be embraced, as a new battle to be won. That is how they get more experienced and better prepared to react, if the same thing happens again.

Poor people watch TV a lot and/or are into sports

> *"Rich people have small TVs and big libraries, and poor people have small libraries and big TVs."*
>
> ***Zig Ziglar***

Everyone knows that time is money. Poor people tend to spend their time without getting anything in return. The entertainment business generates its wealth by using the time poor people spend watching their favorite programs and commercials.

If we watch a sports event, what can we change? The answer is – nothing. What happens is that we waste our precious time. Time that could be used better – with our family, with our friends, to develop ourselves, to learn something new, to read a book, etc. Poor people literally spend their time, making money for someone else. In contrast, rich people seldom watch television and prefer to play sports instead of watching it.

We consider the following **Dean Kamen's** quote relevant here:

> **"I do not want to waste any time. And if you are not working on important things, you are wasting time."**

Poor people do not care about their health

> *"The foundation of success in life is good health: that is the substratum fortune; it is also the basis of happiness. A person cannot accumulate a fortune very well when he is sick."*
>
> ***P. T. Barnum***

Poor people prefer not to eat healthy, they do not go regularly for medical check-ups and they do not do sports. They disregard the well-known fact that if a person is not healthy, he or she cannot perform 100%. This is one of the reasons why, although we all have 24 hours a day, some achieve a lot more compared to others.

Rich people always find time to look after their health. By going for prophylactic medical examinations, rich people could be diagnosed with a certain disease in its early stages. Thus, they can be cured easier, faster and cheaper. On the other hand, poor people often go to the doctor only when it is too late. Hence, they spend a lot more time and money.

Also, the ambition to work very hard, as good as it is, should not put our health at risk. Having enough time to rest helps our body and mind recover. That increases our creativity and productivity.

In short, no matter how poor or rich we currently are, we should take good care of our health.

Poor people live in the past

> ***"I have realized that the past and future are real illusions, that they exist in the present, which is what there is and all there is."***
>
> ***Alan W. Watts***

Generally speaking, we tend to keep in our memory a better version of the past than it actually was. Despite all difficulties and setbacks, we cherish the moments of joy and success and remember them longer. All that is normal, because it helps us remain positive about our life. Past achievements inspire us to unveil our full potential in the future. However, this is just one side of the coin. The other, unfortunately, is related to idealizing the past to the extent that we are not comfortable with living in the present anymore. Such a notion could put our self-development at risk.

When talking to poor people, we can notice that they speak a lot about how everything was so much better before and how awful things are in the present. Rich people, for their part, do not live in the past. They work hard in the present, in order to provide for a better future.

Poor people think that nothing ever changes around them. Rich people know that the world is constantly changing. They understand that managing the change and being flexible are two very important skills and they work hard on improving them every day.

Poor people do not use their strengths

"There is an amazing power getting to know your inner self and learning how to use it and not fight with the world. If you know what makes you happy, your personality, interests and capabilities, just use them, and everything else flows beautifully."

Juhi Chawla

If we are not good at math but we are great in learning new languages, what will we do? Poor people will try to improve their math knowledge, so that they can reach an average level at it. Certainly, that has a side effect: the time spent on math lessons would allow them to develop their strength (learning languages) no more than the average level as well. Rich people, on the other hand, will focus on their strength and maximize the result.

If we hate math but still reach average level of knowledge at it, would we take a career that is mostly based on our math skills? Even if we find a highly paid job, we will most probably hate it. This will generate stress and dissatisfaction. Now think what would happen if we can develop our strength and work what we love and what we are good at – would we feel happier? There is no need to answer this question – we all know it is better to do something we love than something we hate. Having that in mind, we are convinced that everyone has come across the saying:

***"Choose a job you love,
and you will never have to work
a day in your life."***

But then again, this is exactly the mistake most of the poor people make – they work something they really hate their entire life. If that is the case, it is obvious that a change is necessary. We have to realize that only by using our strengths to the max, will we be able win the money making game.

Poor people don't treat money as a tool, but rather as a goal

"Money is only a tool. It will take you wherever you wish, but it will not replace you as the driver."

Ayn Rand

That is mainly because poor people don't understand the basic money principles. In short, today's money tends to lose relatively fast over time some of its important characteristics, such as purchasing power and store of value, much faster than the coins made of gold or silver that people used centuries ago.

Let's take professional sport as an example: Half a century ago, a top-level football player could be bought for less than a million dollars. Today the stars are being transferred between the clubs for $100-, $150- and even over $200 million. Now imagine that 50 years ago we were one of these stars. If we hadn't invested somehow our, say, $600000, we would have ended up with no money for our retirement.

We need to ask ourselves: is any of today's star players 200 times better than their colleagues from the past, to cost 200 times more? Certainly not. To get this story right, we must

compare money not in nominal but in real terms. To do that, economists use a number of indicators:
- Purchasing power parity;
- Cumulative inflation for the period;
- Price indexes;
- Consumer basket of goods;
- etc.

After doing the calculations, we can conclude: it is not that the star player costs 200 times more – it is the money that have lost a huge amount of value (compared to 50 years ago).

If we don't find a way to multiply the money we make today, we risk becoming poor tomorrow. And that is exactly what rich people realize and take appropriate action against. Getting the money is merely the start of their journey. From that moment on they use it as a tool for achieving their current and future goals.

Poor people do not work towards making the world a better place, as they don't care about it

"Most people yearn to contribute, make the world a better place and have success.... all at the same time... Make sure to give your business a background, a mission and a story.

*That might be the most important step part of any venture.
And remember, giving may be the best investment you ever make."*

Blake Mycoskie

Generally speaking, poor people are not interested in global development or different visions for the future but rather in trivial everyday topics. They are more likely to believe conspiracy theories and fake news because they rarely use high-quality information sources. Poor people fall into the misconception that they are too small and insignificant to have an impact on the world.

The truth is: every person is like a piece in the puzzle - there is a special place for each of us in the big picture. Sometimes even a small thing can make a huge difference - sadly, this is seldom realized by the poor.

On the other hand, there is a great number of examples that once the rich build their wealth, they start doing something to improve the wellbeing of others – charity work, financing of scientific research, finding cure for incurable diseases, etc. As a matter of fact, rich people are the ones that move mankind forward.

2. Main factors preventing poor people from becoming rich

"The gap between the rich and poor is widening fast."

Richard Rogers

We cannot get rich, without making an effort. All of the above issues can be merged in the following:
- Afraid of change;
- Have bad time management;
- Lose motivation fast;
- Spend their money without budget planning and with no tracking of their expenses;
- Get in debt;
- Work for money instead of making the money work for them.

Afraid of change

"We are afraid of ideas, of experimenting, of change. We shrink from thinking a problem through to a logical conclusion."

Anne Sullivan

So many books and articles pay attention to the so called "comfort zone" and rightly so. Sometimes we might find it hard to get out of it and that can slow us down in our quest to become rich. Every change on personal and professional level generates additional stress and provokes us to resist it. The fear of the unknown can dominate over the better prospects that the change offers. However, the more experienced we are, the less we are likely to let our emotions decide instead of us.

We need to realize that in life nothing is permanent. That will make it possible for us to be open to changes and accept them as important factors for our progress. In today's world the ability to manage change is one of the most important skills that we should develop in order to be successful. The time when the strongest wins is long gone. If we are to become winners, we need to be able to manage the changes and be flexible.

Bad time management

"You know, you only get to live life once, so there are two things that that yields. One is that there's no point in crying over spilt milk, but secondly you hate

wasting time, energy, and whatever talent you've got."

David Miliband

Our success or failure is directly linked with the ability to manage our time. It includes optimizing our schedule, setting up deadlines, prioritizing tasks, avoiding the waste of time and saving some of it for family, friends and rest. All that has to be in line with our individual characteristics, habits and peculiarities.

For example, we all know that, depending on the time of the day when a person is more productive, he or she can be categorized as either a morning or an evening person. Having that in mind, it makes no sense to expect great achievements at work from an evening person early in the morning (this is the best time for them to relax).

Whatever we do, we must not forget that our most valuable asset is time. Each day we all have the same amount of it and it is up to us to utilize it efficiently. Certainly, those who manage their time best will be greatly rewarded and those who waste it will lag behind. If we belong to the latter, the first step to improve our daily routine is to identify the time wasters and remove them one by one. It might not be easy at first but soon we will see the good results and that will motivate us to be even more time-efficient.

Lose motivation fast

"People often say that motivation doesn't last. Well, neither does bathing – that's why we recommend it daily."

Zig Ziglar

All we do in our lives starts with passion and motivation - in return for our actions we expect a certain positive outcome. However, it is often the case that even the strongest motivation does not last very long. The initial situation can change, unexpected problems can appear and our attitude or expectations can also change as a result. Suddenly we find the goal not so attractive and we quit - this is a typical example of lost motivation.

Thus, as much as we need motivation in the beginning of our new ventures, we also have to try and turn it into habit, in order to last long enough to reach our goal. One way of doing so is to divide our main goal into multiple smaller goals that can be fulfilled a lot faster. Reaching the first one will make us happy and confident to go on to the second one, then to the third, etc. - just like climbing a ladder step by step.

Having a realistic approach towards our projects is also vital for our motivation. A deep research and analysis of relevant data will give us a clear picture of the risks and opportunities we are facing. That will prevent us from being too over excited or too skeptical about the project (both these emotions could spoil our motivation quickly).

Spend their money without budget planning and with no tracking of their expenses

"I see good personal financial management as setting – and keeping – a budget."

John Rampton

A common mistake of the poor people is that they do not realize how important it is to manage their incoming and outgoing money flows. They often buy things they don't really need that prove to be too expensive for them. Therefore, they let money slip through their fingers and are not able to accumulate wealth.

In order to win the money making game, we have to track our income and expenses and make sure we take control of our personal finances. Creating our own budget is the first thing to do in the process of building wealth. It is safe to say that time spent on our budget is directly related to the progress we make in getting richer.

In short, budget planning improves our financial discipline and puts us in charge of our money. It is instrumental of the long term success of our financial strategy.

Get in debt

"A man in debt is so far a slave."

Ralph Waldo Emerson

Poor people want everything at the moment and they are ready to get in debt just to fulfil their needs, disregarding the consequences. We have to do our best not to act in such an irresponsible way because, more often than not, getting out of debt proves to be very hard.

Using somebody else's money means that in addition to paying it back we will be charged a certain amount of interest and fees. Sometimes, especially when talking about consumer loans, we might even end up owing twice as much money as we have originally borrowed. In other words, with our decision we make it possible for the bank to accumulate quite a big profit at our expense.

Therefore, we must be extremely careful when we intend to take a loan and we should ask ourselves - do we really need it, what impact will it have on our budget and how long will it take to pay it back?

Whatever the answers are, one thing is certain - by getting in debt we miss the opportunity to use our money for something else (rather than paying back the debt). Furthermore, we are not talking about money that we currently have (otherwise we wouldn't have taken the loan) but about money that we should earn in the future.

Work for money instead of making the money work for them

"The rich don't work for money – the rich invent money."

Robert Kiyosaki

Last but not least, if we are determined to become wealthy, we have to start multiplying the money we make. We need to learn how to invest in order to gradually overcome our dependence on the next paycheck and achieve a higher standard of living. To invest our money means that, instead of spending it, we put it in certain projects, securities, goods, items, properties, etc., that we expect to increase in value over time.

In order for our investment to be successful, those expectations must be based on facts. Investing in what we know nothing about is no different than taking a shot in the dark. Therefore, before making the investment, we should gather as much information as possible. It has to be up-to-date and to come from reliable sources. Once we finish with our research, we are ready to invest, being confident that our choice is rational.

Now is the time to underline that there are no such things as guaranteed profits and risk-free investments. In a market economy we should always anticipate trend changes and learn to adapt our decisions to them.

In the following chapters there are some ideas and guidance on how to improve our way of thinking and move in the right direction on the path to wealth.

3. Changing our mindset and habits

"Good habits are the key to all success. Bad habits are the unlocked door to failure."

Og Mandino

Bad habits are dragging us backwards and prevent us from getting the most out of our daily routine. We should not wait for bad habits to grow within us, we need to drop them while we still can, or otherwise they will get control over us.

Below are listed several pieces of advice which could be useful in our strive to become more effective and efficient:

- We need to stop procrastinating;
- We must stop thinking like bank customers, we need to think like the bank;
- If something is not working, we should try something new;
- We shouldn't wait for others to help us reach our goals and to make our dreams come true;
- We must choose our friends carefully;
- We shouldn't take advice from unsuccessful people;

- We must reduce our reliance on credit cards;
- We need to stop complaining and being negative;
- We shouldn't think that we know it all;
- We must constantly educate ourselves;
- We need to learn to control our emotions;
- We must accept that we cannot always win.

We need to stop procrastinating

"Procrastination is the bad habit of putting off until the day after tomorrow what should have been done the day before yesterday."

Napoleon Hill

On one hand, that is not to postpone important tasks and wait till the last minute to complete them. By doing so we risk falling in a trap that is not so easy to get out of, because:

- Work keeps piling up;
- Deadlines are pushing us harder and harder;
- While trying to finish the multiple tasks in time, we might forget some of them;

- The quality of our performance may decline, etc.

On the other hand, that is not to spend much time on social media, reality shows and sports on TV, computer games, etc. We must admit there are so many distractions in our everyday life that if we do not learn how to ignore them, we risk losing our concentration completely. That would reduce our productivity and stop us from achieving our goals.

Having all that in mind, we don't have to quit doing all the fun stuff. After all, they helps us to relax, blow some steam off and recharge. However, we need to impose certain limits upon those rather time-consuming activities, in order not to let them distract us or even prevent us from doing work.

We must stop thinking like bank customers, we need to think like the bank

"We all get so caught up in the moment of what we're doing every day, it's hard to hit that reset button and get pulled away from all that and see life from a different perspective."

Tony Stewart

In other words, don't go with the flow – be in the driver's seat instead. Banks offer a number of products such as loans, deposits, credit cards, investment plans, etc., with the sole purpose to maximize their profit. Can we follow their example? Of course we can - we just have to find our niche and benefit from it.

In today's consumerist society, it is a matter of personal choice whether we wait for others to offer solutions to all our problems (and, of course, to make us pay for them), or we decide to be the ones providing those solutions.

We'd better be the bank than the customer, right? To make it happen, we need to have competitive advantages over other people, meaning that our skills and expertise have to be superior to theirs. This can be certainly achieved with proper motivation and hard work - to be able to take, we have to give first.

When talking about money, we must know the difference between spending it and investing it. Let us highlight that every time we spend money, we make somebody else rich.

If something is not working, we should try something new

> *"Everybody else is afraid to fail. I do not really care because when I fail, I try something new."*
>
> *Vinod Khosla*

We simply cannot expect new results by doing the same things over and over again. We must learn to change. Easier said than done, right? Most people tend to be afraid to get out of their comfort zone. That makes sense – if we are doing well, why change? But on how many occasions have we asked ourselves questions like:
- Can I do better?
- Is this the best job for me?
- Have I reached my peak?
- Is there anything new I can learn after so much time spent with the same company?

After we find the answers to such questions, we could sit down, analyze the facts and make the so called informed decision about our future.

Shockingly, many people are not even willing to get out of their zone of total discomfort – that's a serious risk-related issue. A person, not ready to take risks is more likely to accept the unfavorable current situation, rather than go ahead and change it.

From a psychological point of view, the easiest thing to do is to scare somebody off. It is a lot harder to persuade the individual to be proactive and to believe in the high potential of a new venture. Let us highlight that it is perfectly normal for one to be afraid. Fear helps us to survive when in danger. All that is brilliantly summed up in a famous **Nelson Mandela** quote:

"I learned that courage was not the absence of fear, but the triumph over it. The brave man is not he who does not feel afraid, but he who conquers that fear."

We shouldn't wait for others to help us to reach our goals and to make our dreams come true

"If you want a thing done well, do it ourselves."

Napoleon Bonaparte

Now this is a tricky one. The point is that in life we follow our own path. We meet many people along the way – friends, enemies, loved ones, colleagues, mentors, etc. But by no means should we hold any of them responsible for our success or failure. We can consult with them, ask for their opinion but at the same time we should be aware that there is no such thing as collective responsibility – it is always personal. We are the ones to call the shots, benefit from the good choices and lose from the bad ones.

Being an excellent team worker, finding wise teachers and following instructions does not contradict with the above. After all, this is how we gain valuable experience and develop both professionally and personally. Moreover, as **Sam Levenson** suggested:

> *"Learn from other people's mistakes. Life is too short to make them all ourselves"*

We don't have to "invent the wheel" but, based on our talent and competence, to set realistic goals and to be determined to accomplish them. Having that in mind, we must be ready and willing to write down our own history as no one else will do it for us.

Choose our friends carefully

"Show me your friends and I will tell you who you are."

That makes sense because the people we call friends are the ones that share our understanding of life in general, our interests, hobbies, role-models and often - our social status.

Various studies and social experiments have proven that if our four closest friends are poor, most probably we are or will end up being poor too. Therefore, if we are serious about winning the money making game, we need to stop surrounding ourselves with poor people.

The intellectual capacity of our friends is not to be underestimated as well. We shall refer here to another saying:

"If you are the smartest person in the room, you are in the wrong room."

This wise quote encourages us to always look for self-improvement and discover our maximum potential. In this regard, being friends with hard-working, smart and ambitious people will definitely have a positive influence on us.

We shouldn't take advice from unsuccessful people

"Successful people are always looking for opportunities to help others. Unsuccessful people are always asking – 'What's in it for me?'"

Brian Tracy

Instead, we must find someone who has done what we want to do and take advice from them. After all, he or she is living proof that our goal is reachable. It would be even better if they share with us their success story, so that we can get the whole picture. That doesn't mean we have to blindly follow their instructions - we might not be in the same situation or simply would like to choose a different approach. Either way, a good example is always welcome - it will motivate us and give us food for thought. On the other hand, we should do our best to avoid taking advice from our friends or relatives on topics they know nothing about. Without a doubt, it is a big mistake to mix our feelings and emotions with business. Moreover, since we trust our friends, we are often unable to realize how bad their pieces of advice might be for us.

Let us highlight once again that no matter whose advice we decide to take, the result of our actions is solely our responsibility.

We must reduce our reliance on credit cards

"Credit cards are like snakes: Handle 'em long enough, and one will bite you."

Elizabeth Warren

Try and limit their utilization as much as possible. Bear in mind that the credit limit we have on our card is not our money anyway, i.e. if we spend it, then we must pay back more, as interest and various fees apply. Compared to other credit products, such as overdrafts, personal and home loans, credit cards normally have the highest interest rate which makes them one of the most expensive forms of credit. Also, with a credit card it is harder to track our spending (with the majority of loans we know in advance exactly how much money we need) and therefore we risk to buy a lot of unnecessary things. The best-case scenario is that we keep our credit card full and use it mostly in the event of force majeure.

Another smart way to manage our credit card is to utilize it only for those payments, that fall within the grace period (when we are charged no interest) and pay them back in full before that period expires. In the following chapters we shall address the topic in more detail.

We need to stop complaining and being negative

"There comes a certain point in life when you have to stop blaming other people for how you feel or the misfortunes in your life. You cannot go through life obsessing about what might have been."

Hugh Jackman

Blaming somebody else for our failures is simply lying to ourselves. Here comes the question: What can we possibly change, if we do that? There is no point to look for excuses and convenient explanations, as they will not provide any solution to our problems. The same goes for holding other people responsible for how good or bad we cope with the challenges in life.

Every time we face an obstacle, we should not lose heart but mobilize ourselves to overcome it.

It is good to be reminded that our attitude plays a very important role in the process. Negativity will always stand between us and success. Regret, frustration and disappointment are past-oriented emotions that must not be allowed to determine our future. If we consider that and take adequate measures, not only our financial status but our quality of life will improve. Instead of wasting our time and allowing our minds to be occupied by negative thoughts, we should pull ourselves together and get the job done.

We shouldn't think that we know it all

"Develop a passion for learning. If you do, you will never cease to grow."

Anthony J. D'Angelo

It would be a huge mistake, if we believe that we are always right and ignore certain ideas just because they are not ours. There are numerous examples of people with great potential, who fail to succeed due to their stubbornness and uncooperativeness. To avoid that, we must not confuse self-confidence with self-sufficiency.

Also, doing something the same way over and over again does not mean this is the only way or the best way for it to be done. In other words, we should be open-minded and ready to take into consideration different suggestions, viewpoints, opinions, approaches, etc., as they enrich our experience. However, listening to them does not equate to accepting and automatically following them.

No matter what our profession or area of expertise is, we could benefit from a discussion (or even an argument) with other specialists. Their way of thinking may draw our attention to facts and circumstances that we have somehow overlooked and inspire us to take innovative and creative decision.

We must constantly educate ourselves

"It's really not about the money. It's just about educating ourselves."

Lisa Leslie

We live in a constantly changing world. The technological boom has drastically influenced both, our work and lifestyle, and it will continue to do so in the future. The vast majority of job occupations we know today are most likely to disappear in the next couple of decades. Along with that, new jobs, requiring new sets of skills, will be created.

So, what qualities should we have to be successful in the near future? In order to be part of progress, we must be flexible, adaptive and embrace change. The best way to do it: to never stop educating ourselves. Every good opportunity to take classes, read and attend seminars should be used. There are no cheats, no shortcuts and no immediate results - we must have the patience to make these small steps each day. The extra knowledge will broaden our horizons and will certainly give us a competitive edge over the persons who do not possess it. Therefore, we can consider it a long-term investment in ourselves. In this regard, we would like to point out that our personal development is closely interrelated with the process of lifelong learning.

We need to learn to control our emotions

"If you don't control your emotions, your emotions will control your acts, and that's not good."

Mariano Rivera

High emotions tend to lower our money making capacity. Some of the latest studies in the field of economics have reached to the conclusion that human behavior is irrational more often than not. As such, it is hard to be predicted and explained by the traditional economic models. They are based on the assumption that people always take their decision, aiming to maximize results and minimize expenses.

On a number of occasions though, a human being would react oppositely to the sound economic logic due to his/her emotional status (good or bad mood, anger, joy, anxiety, over- or underestimation of the situation, etc.).

Certainly, we cannot expect good results from poor decisions. Unfortunately, some of them may have long-lasting negative effects on our personal finances, that could move us further from our goals. For that reason, we are advised to keep our head cool even in the most critical moments and not to allow our judgement to be distracted by irrelevant thoughts or emotions. In other words, we have to raise our emotional intelligence.

We must accept that we cannot always win

"You cannot win unless you learn how to lose."
Kareem Abdul-Jabbar

We have to learn how to lose – winners are not afraid of losing. For the development of a winning mindset, it is crucial to do our best every time, even in the worst circumstances. After all, we are not the masters of the universe, many things are out of our control and that is absolutely fine as long as we remain true to ourselves. A famous quote by **Winston Churchill** teaches us that:

"Success consists of going from failure to failure without loss of enthusiasm."

Along these lines, as much as failure defeats losers, it inspires winners. Let us highlight that if we are a hundred percent determined to pursue our aims and objectives, the setbacks have no chance to discourage us. We could refer to another great man's wise words on the subject – **Albert Einstein**:

"In the middle of difficulty lies opportunity."

With all being said so far, it is of key importance to point out that each and every move we make requires certain amount of time and takes away some of our energy – both physically and mentally. It is no coincidence that when we want to show our gratitude to someone, we usually say:

"Thank you for your time and effort!"

Let's take a moment to think about the meaning behind this expression. Time and effort go hand in hand as determinants of success and we have to make optimal use of them. We will soon realize that getting rid of our bad habits equals to freeing up our day and devoting it to the ultimate goal – winning the money making game.

CHANGE MANAGEMENT

"Progress is impossible without change, and those who cannot change their minds cannot change anything."

George Bernard Shaw

When we speak about change we often hear the common English expression purported to be a translation of a traditional Chinese curse:
"May you live in interesting times"

Change is one of the few constants in our life. Change is all around us and with time we see that it is happening faster and faster. It can provoke uncertainty in our lives and that can be a very stressful experience.

Change challenges our abilities to overcome difficulties and tests how flexible we are. The way we handle change makes a huge difference in our emotional health and well-being. Change is a synonym of growth and we have to understand that, in order to be more successful, we need to change our ways of doing things when they are not going in the direction we want them to go.

"Without change there is no innovation, creativity, or incentive for improvement. Those who initiate change will have a better opportunity to manage the change that is inevitable."

William Pollard

It is important to mention that growth is a process - not a one-off activity. Although most of us probably realize that fact, we do not usually have the time to stop and realistically assess where we are now and where we want to be in the future.

Let us take into consideration this popular quote by ***Lewis Carroll:***

"If you don't know where you are going, any road will get you there."

The first step of our growth process is to determine our starting position. Next, we need to think if we should continue in the same direction and if we keep on doing the things we are doing right now, where we would find ourselves in the future. Most probably, we will conclude that it won't be our dream location.

In this case, the key to our personal growth is to be able to choose another path. We have to understand that we cannot change our starting point, but we can choose where we want to head to next.

To begin the changing process, we must be convinced that it is the right time to do it. We can reach such a conclusion either through honest self-assessment or through certain new circumstances in our life. Of course, the first one is the better option, however people normally decide to make a change in their life when something unexpected happens.

Once we reach to this point, we have two choices yet again:

- Do nothing. This is what most people prefer as it is much easier, although it won't take them where they want to be;
- Take a completely different approach and change.

In order to see why most people prefer the easier way and why only the ones with the right motivation succeed in life, we have to understand the change management concept as a whole.

> *"Doing what you want to do is easy. Doing what you have to do is hard."*
>
> ***Larry Elder***

So what is change management?

Change management is a very powerful tool used mainly by companies to guide new processes and restructures within the organization. From individual perspective understanding change will help us realize why we act in a specific way when we need to start doing new things in our life. Every change comes with completely new set of challenges that we must handle and always includes a mix of emotions.

Everyone is going through similar emotions through the change process. Knowing the psychology behind our behavior will make the implementation of changes easier, will reduce stress and will help us to achieve happiness in the long run.

> *"No one is in control of your happiness but you; therefore, you*

have the power to change anything about ourselves or your life that you want to change."

Barbara De Angelis

Nowadays, change is an inevitable part of our life and if we really want to win the money making game, we should have understanding of the way it works. Change often alters our routine, challenges our perceptions and makes us reflect on how things are done.

Faced with something new or unexpected, our initial reaction is usually one of anxiety and sometimes – fear.

Lack of knowledge how change makes us feel is a very common reason why people tend to fail when pursuing happiness.

As far as money is concerned, the greater the level of control we have over our earnings, the happier we are likely to be.

"I cannot change the direction of the wind, but I can adjust my sails to always reach my destination."

Jimmy Dean

In this chapter we will talk about change in the context of moving towards rich people's way of thinking.

1. The change curve

"You have to change the set, stay ahead of the curve."

Carson Daly

In order to understand change and the stages associated with it, we will go through the Kubler-Ross grief curve.

The Kubler-Ross grief curve describes the 5 stages of grief by a model consisting of the various levels or stages of emotions, experienced by a person who is close to death or is a survivor of an intimate death.

The 5 stages included in the model are:
- Shock and Denial;
- Anger;
- Bargaining;
- Depression;
- Acceptance.

This model was introduced by - and named after Elisabeth Kubler-Ross in her book called 'Death and Dying' which came out in 1969. The concept of the model was broadly accepted, and its validity was proven in the majority of cases and situations related to change. Since then, it has been widely utilized as a method of helping people understand their reactions to significant change or upheaval. Most of the stages described by Kubler-Ross are completely subconscious. Also, some people move very quickly through them, compared to others.

Here comes the question – how does all this apply to building wealth? It is quite easy actually – we prefer to stay in our comfort zone, although it is not taking us anywhere.

Let's go through the different phases:

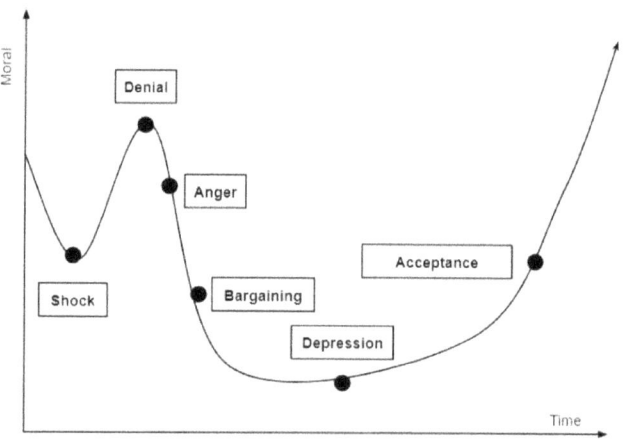

The following are brief descriptions of each of the 5 stages:

- Shock and Denial – This is a phase during which one puts on a temporary defense mechanism and takes time to process reality.
- Anger – The next stage is often associated with anger. At this point we come to the realization that change is not optional. We may look for someone to blame. At this stage we might feel isolated, apathetic and even depressed.
- Bargaining – When the stage of anger passes away, one may start thinking about ways to postpone the inevitable and try to find out the best thing left in the situation.
- Depression – At this stage we tend to feel sadness, fear, regret, guilt and other negative emotions.
- Acceptance – Finally, we find out for ourselves the meaning behind the necessity of making the change, we stop resisting and move ahead with it.

Each of these five stages can last for a different period of time. Moreover, it is possible for a person to get stuck in a particular stage and be unable to get out of it.

2. Change management bias

"I think unconscious bias is one of the hardest things to get at."

Ruth Bader Ginsburg

As change management plays a very important part in reaching our goals, we also need to get rid of the most common bias that we come across when talking about change:
- Change is optional;
- Change happens quickly;
- Solutions must be perfect from the first time;
- Resistance is a bad sign;
- Old dogs cannot learn new tricks.

Change is optional

"There is nothing permanent except change."

Heraclitus

We have two choices – stay where we are and be poor or start changing ourselves, in order to self-develop and win the money-making game. It makes no sense to go with the first one, right? If we aim to become high achievers, we need to keep moving forward. That is why we don't really consider change optional. It makes it possible for us to improve our quality of life and take advantage of the many good opportunities we are offered. Change is natural and happens all the time. If we are afraid of it or reject it, someone else will profit from it. Refusing to become part of the change, we will lag behind and may find it hard to catch up.

The same logic applies to building wealth - a certain asset that was the best investment 5 or 10 years ago might prove to be the worst investment today. In the meantime, a multitude of brand new investment assets have emerged - we have to find out whether some of them would bring in a better return than ours. If that is the case, we are left with no other option but to change our investment strategy.

Change happens quickly

"Life is short and progress is slow."

Gabriel Lippmann

It is true that sometimes our life can change in a matter of seconds (for example, due to a major natural disaster). However, our book aims to focus on the positive change we all need, in order to win the money-making game. That type of change could be managed, as it is mostly related to our motivation, attitude and mindset. Having taken the decision to change, we must act to put it in practice. Setting our strategic direction and following it are two equally important tasks. In this regard, we should know that becoming rich is not a fast process and we need to be patient to get the right results.

Also, when talking about "quick" and "slow" or "rich" and "poor", different people mean different things. That's why we should learn to clearly formulate and objectively assess our goals and achievements. For example, "I want to be rich soon" is nothing but a good wish, while "I want to increase my net wealth by 15 % in 6 months" is a well-defined goal, as the latter includes a target amount of money and a fixed deadline. That allows us to measure our progress and act accordingly.

Solutions must be perfect from the first time

"By trying to advance the perfect conservative solution, nobody wins."

Bill Flores

Most probably we will fail to set up a perfect plan from the first time. By no means is this a reason to quit and never try again. In order to eventually succeed, we must remain positive and believe in ourselves.

So many of the world's most distinguished businessmen, actors, musicians, athletes, etc. share that it took them years to make the breakthrough to success. Some of them were told a number of times that they would never make it, got rejected and even laughed at, but they did not get discouraged by the initial failure. Instead, they kept trying and trying until they got credit for their efforts.

There is one thing in common between all these people, regardless of their occupation - they have managed to find their *ikigai* (*from Japanese - "a reason for being"*). According to this concept, *ikigai* is the intersection of our profession, mission, passion and vocation. Certainly, striking such a perfect balance is no easy task but when we accomplish it, we will feel its positive impact on all aspects of our life.

Resistance is a bad sign

"The path of least resistance is the path of the loser."

H. G. Wells

Resistance is not a bad thing, but the sooner we understand the meaning of change, the faster we will reach our goal. In this regard, we have to make sure that our decision to change is well thought out. Frequent changes might prove to be even worse than status quo. Therefore, we ought to develop our critical thinking skills, analyze and compare the potential results of our actions.

When speaking of individual resistance, we must be aware that it is caused by our habits, routine, inconvenience, past security and fear of the unknown. It is a well-known fact that, due to the factors mentioned above, different people react differently in similar situation. Moreover, we all have limits and certain "red lines" that we are not willing to cross.

In conclusion, we would like to reiterate that being resistant to change is a normal behavior that might not be very easy to overcome. Knowing this, we should be able to differentiate the emotional from the logical side of change. Once we do that, we are ready to make the first step in the right direction.

Old dogs cannot learn new tricks

We should not be fooled by this common misconception. Nobody is too young or too old to learn something new. All the extra knowledge acquired prepares us better for the changes in our lives. It helps us confront our fears, false beliefs and negative thoughts.

In order to improve ourselves professionally, we need to follow the latest developments (scientific, legal, technological, practical, etc.) in our area of expertise. There is a reason to be positive about it: nowadays our access to information is many times easier than it was in the past and we have only ourselves to blame, if we don't use it in the best possible way.

Finally, let us take a look at the following quote by ***Confucius***:

"It is only the wisest and the stupidest that cannot change."

So if we do not belong to any of those two groups, we should stop looking for excuses and embrace change. It is good to remember that we can never overcome a challenge by denying it. Instead, we have to tackle it with self-confidence and determination.

3. Change management and money making

Let us explain what stages we go through when we change the way we manage our money.

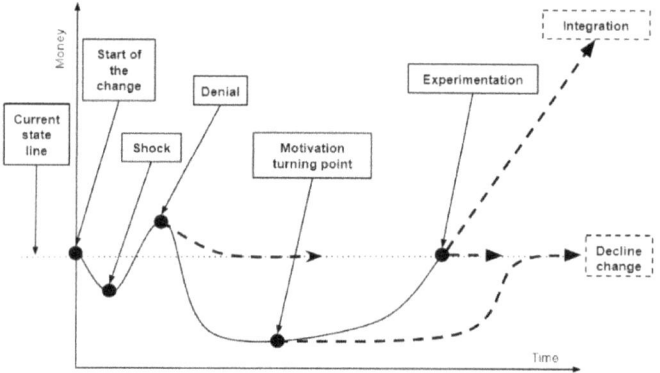

In the figure above, we have Time on the x-axis and Money on the y-axis.
The current state line shows the way we manage the money (normally from paycheck to paycheck). It has a big influence on us - every time we try to move away from it, the current state line tends to bring us back. This is

because it represents the upper border of our comfort zone. The more time we live in the comfort zone, the more difficult it will be for us to change, since we develop habits that are hard to break.

Statistically this line represents how ⅔ of the world's population manage their money. If we are among those people and decide that we want to be more successful and to improve our wealth, then we need to start the change process.

This process can be summarized into the following stages:
- Start of the change;
- Shock;
- Denial;
- Motivation turning point;
- Experimentation;
- Implementation.

3.1 Starting the change

"If you want to change attitudes, start with a change in behavior."

William Glasser

This stage is closely related to the problem-solving and decision-making process. In other words, we start the change when we see that there is a problem and we want to find a solution for it. Good timing is crucial for the positive effect of the change we are about to make. We will come back to it in the chapter dedicated to Time Management.

Below is a basic problem-solving and decision-making model that we might follow during this initial stage:

- Defining the problem and the decision that needs to be made;
- Gathering information and analyzing the problem;
- Generating potential solutions, comparing the different options and making a decision.
- Selecting the best solution and implementing the decision.

Defining the problem and the decision that needs to be made

"You don't fix the problem until you define it."

John W. Snow

It involves examining the situation and identifying the core issues or problems at the heart of it. We usually start looking to improve our way of managing money when:

- We live from paycheck to paycheck.
- We are constantly borrowing money from friends and family.
- We have a lot of debt.
- Our money is gone long before the end of the month.
- We want to earn more money.

These are all symptoms that a deviation exists between our goals and actions:

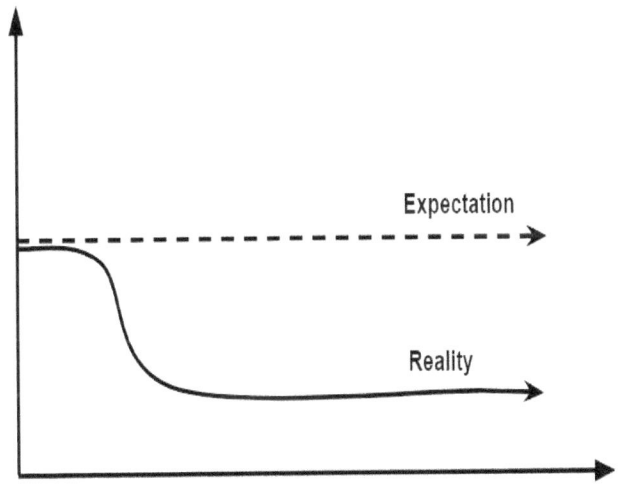

Having defined the problem, we can go ahead and define the decision - to close the gap, illustrated by the figure above.

Gathering information and analyzing the problem

"We cannot solve our problems with the same thinking we used when we created them."

Albert Einstein

This stage should not to be underestimated, as it provides the basis for our financial planning. After we have defined the problem and the decision needed, it is time to examine them in detail. This can only be done with the help of relevant and up-to date information. In our case, it is related to the money we make and spend.

In order to straighten out our finances, we have to learn how to create a personal monthly budget. The good news: this task can be accomplished relatively fast and is not at all difficult. It might involve consulting sources such as:
- Paychecks and documentation;
- Account balances;
- Bills;
- Loan and credit card statements;
- etc.

After we collect and summarize all the information concerning our incomes and expenditures, we should analyze it thoroughly. The analysis will help us identify which of our incoming and outgoing money flows could be optimized.

We will discuss the matter in more depth in the chapter dedicated to creating our first budget.

Generating potential solutions, comparing the different options and making a decision

"We have to be about finding long-term solutions to our biggest challenges."

Bill Haslam

When we have got a budget put in place, we should figure out what its problematic spots are and start looking for potential solutions. Are we able to save money? Do we need an extra income source? Do we overspend? Are we in debt? During this stage our aim is to identify the options that are available, play out different scenarios and make a decision.

It is likely that we will find several options to choose from. Now is the time to compare their advantages and disadvantages, in order to pick the best one.

The research conducted at the information-gathering stage might suggest that a certain course of action should be taken or avoided. Alternatively, a new set of solutions might present itself at this point. Sometimes the right decision could be a combination of the options considered. Without question, our analytical skills will gradually improve over time, as a result of the efforts made.

Selecting the best solution and implementing the decision

"The best solutions are often simple, yet unexpected."

Julian Casablancas

Once we have identified all the potential solutions, we need to select the one we think is the best and start working on its implementation. In order to measure our progress, we have to determine our short-term, midterm and long-term goals and set the respective deadlines for meeting them. If the outcome matches our expectations, we are on the right track to winning the money making game.

It is important to know that we might not be able to choose the best solution on the first try. This should not discourage us and we just have to look for alternatives until we find the one that works.

Having briefly described the problem-solving and decision-making model, let us come back to the psychological aspects of change. As soon as we decide to change, we will face the first two stages of the process – Shock and Denial. As stated earlier, this is the time when the individual is put on a temporary defense mechanism and it takes a while for his or her brain to process reality.

3.2 Shock stage

"Just as the body goes into shock after a physical trauma, so does the human psyche go into shock after the impact of a major loss."

Anne Grant

It is often caused by a mismatch between expectations and reality combined with the fear of new things. For example, if we decide to improve our personal finances, we may have to completely change our current routine and that could be quite stressful at the beginning. Moreover, we may feel afraid of not being able to cope with the new way of handling money.

Normally, Shock is the shortest stage. It might continue from several hours to several days. Curiously enough, it is common to experience not only anxiety or but also happiness before moving to the denial phase.

- Anxiety occurs in the beginning of the change process. In most cases, this is because we do not know how things will play out after the change. At this stage we realize on a subconscious level that the change and the following events lie beyond our control and do not fit within the borders of our comfort zone. In these cases anxiety is based on the fact that we are unable to picture what the future will be after the change.
- On the other hand, we may also experience happiness during this phase. We could feel this way if we firmly believe change is necessary and if other people share our opinion about it. Furthermore, there will be a sense of relief that the old system is finally going to be changed for the better. In other

words, happiness is a result of the feeling that things will not continue to be done as before.

When we make the decision to start managing our money more efficiently and effectively, we should take under consideration that different types of people need different amount of time to get the right results (depending on whether or not they embrace change quickly).

What we must do is take as much time as needed and obtain as much information on the subject as possible. If we are determined to change our way of handling money, it is good to start our journey by setting and accomplishing short term goals, so that we can give our subconscious mind the assurance that there is nothing to be afraid of and change is necessary.

3.3 Denial stage

"Denial ain't just a river in Egypt."

Mark Twain

It takes time to face up to change. As already mentioned, we might not be ready to accept it right away. The denial stage is based on the

"Change is not necessary" bias and reflects our individual level of resistance to change.

At this phase we often tend to act as if no change is happening. We use the old processes and practices and subconsciously try to convince ourselves the old system that used to work in the past should not be changed.

Without the right self-motivation we can easily get stuck at this stage for a long time and eventually decline change. In other words, depending on our motives to start the change, we may find the Denial stage very easy to pass, while for others it can be impossible to overcome. Here, we often try to persuade ourselves that we can actually fix our money problem without going through all this. It is common to see people start spending less just to prove their point that no change is required and, as a result, their money management improves. However, since they fail to pass the Denial stage, those people would not be able to cross above the "current state" line in the long run.

We can also experience anger that might at first be directed towards the people who suggest we need to change our way of handling money. We start blaming others for the situation that we find ourselves in and for all the stress we have been put upon. At a later point in time, we could realize our mistake and get angry with ourselves.

As mentioned before, this stage corresponds to the part of the change curve in which we are in doubt whether we should go back to our old habits and decline the entire change. Having such thoughts and emotions shows that we subconsciously express anger towards it. That is usually combined with the urge to do everything the old way.

If we fail to move forward from this point, we will return to our comfort zone and we will be back on the "current state" line.

During the Denial stage it is important that we take the time to find out what the change means to us and what its impact on our life could be. Additional thing that we can do at this stage is to try and help other people dealing with the same issue. In our case these could be friends and relatives that are also struggling to handle money effectively. Last but not least, looking at the change from a different angle would certainly be useful and might help us find extra motivation for doing it.

3.4 Motivation turning point stage

"You can look for external sources of motivation and that can catalyze a change, but it won't sustain one. It has to be from an internal desire."

Jillian Michaels

In this stage lies one of the biggest challenges on our path to change - to keep our level of motivation high. We have to realize that motivation is temporary and if it is not strong enough, we might decide to give up change, thus ruining our progress.

During the Motivation turning point phase, the feelings and emotions that can lead to declining the change can be divided into three main categories:
- Disillusionment;
- Depression or Despair;
- Hostility.

Disillusionment

"Wisdom comes by disillusionment."

George Santayana

The first emotion from the list occurs mainly when we feel that our beliefs, values and the goals we set are incompatible with some of the changes taking place. As a result, we become demotivated and the dissatisfaction within increases.

At this point we might also undermine the change by complaining and criticizing. Eventually this can lead to a total rejection of the change. It is important for us to understand that without having the proper motivation (or by completely losing it), we can easily get stuck in this phase.

If we find ourselves in the state of disillusionment, it is important to regain control of the situation as fast as possible.

We can try to pause for a moment, in order to look at the big picture. In cases of disillusionment it is recommended to concentrate on the things that will remain the same even after the change. In other words, to be in control again, we should focus on what will stay intact. This way, by taking a step back to our comfort zone for a while, we will rediscover our motivation and bring it back to a level that will make our passing through this stage easier. Of course, we must have in mind that the approach we described above has nothing to do with going back to the old bad habits that we try to overcome with the entire change process.

Depression and despair

"Life begins on the other side of despair."

Jean-Paul Sartre

The second category from the list is related to the feelings of depression and despair. This is the most difficult phase we can go into and the hardest one to work our way through. If we get ourselves in such situation, we can get stuck in here for a very long period of time. These feelings and emotions are characterized by confusion and, once again, by lack of motivation. Other side effects that can be added here are sadness and apathy. Knowing that this reaction is our subconscious way of expressing the internal fear of what could happen after the change and realizing why we feel ourselves powerless over the change are important factors for overcoming the Depression and despair stage. Furthermore, in our attempt to manage our feelings and emotions better, we could look for new thinking patterns and techniques.

Hostility

> *"He who dreads hostility too much is unfit to rule."*
>
> ***Lucius Annaeus Seneca***

The third emotion from the list is often a result of wrong approach to handling the previous Depression and despair stage. In this phase what we usually feel is hostility. If we come out of the previous stage not being able to control our emotions, that will lead to aggressive behavior towards the people around us. Although the issue is internal, it is human psychology to try and defend ourselves by attacking others. Once again, it is important for us to understand what we are going through and master our emotions.

In short, all these negative feelings can make us completely decline the change. However, if we pass on through this stage and continue with experimenting and implementing the change, we will surely succeed.

3.5 Experimenting stage

> *"We are afraid of ideas, of experimenting, of change. We shrink*

from thinking a problem through to a logical conclusion."

Anne Sullivan

Once we pass the most problematic phase "the motivation turning point", our growth process begins. The key to reaching the experimentation phase is the internal acceptance of change and the ability to control our negative feelings. At this phase we finally give change a real chance and start working without all the negative emotions as we get detached from them. This is the point when we begin to see ourselves as an integral part of the change.

Our confidence returns and we gain control over the situation. This leads to the real implementation of the change. We begin to put some plans in place and create new goals around our desires and wishes. Positive feelings and emotions are coming our way, as we realize that we are doing things right.

It is good to take some time off and reward ourselves for reaching this far after such a long journey. This is the time to feel proud of ourselves because we have just made the first and most important step to our new successful future.

3.6 Implementation stage

"It's important to have a sound idea, but the really important thing is the implementation."

Wilbur Ross

After the implementation stage we will see a big difference in both our emotional and financial status and we will start building our wealth.

This is the point when we begin to accept the new reality that change has created. It is vital to deal with our emotions and force ourselves not to move back to our bad habits from the past.

Once the change is completed, we must make sure we identify, assess and understand what opportunities stand there waiting for us.

In conclusion, remember that change is inevitable. The sooner we accept it, the faster we will get results. Metaphorically speaking, between point A and point B, except for the straight line, there are millions of other connecting lines. It is up to us to decide what kind of line will connect our points A & B, as they are different for each person. Keeping a cool head during the emotional phases described above will determine how long it will take us to win the money making game.

We shouldn't let others to judge us or wait for someone's approval – our success in life is no one else's responsibility. It is important to be in peace with ourselves and be aware of the feelings we are going through during the entire process of change. Understanding their nature is the key to handling them easily.

As a matter of fact, we usually need only one change to completely turn our life around.

TIME MANAGEMENT

"If you don't value your time, neither will others. Stop giving away your time and talents. Value what you know & start charging for it."

Kim Garst

After we make sure we are ready to change ourselves, the next step is to start managing our time more effectively. Feeling constantly busy or overburdened might be a symptom that our time management is not good enough. In this case we need to adjust our schedule and be able to spare the required amount of time to accomplish our goals.

1. Time is money

The biggest asset that we all have is time and we have to learn how to optimally use it. Let's remember the saying: "Time is Money". That is certainly true because no matter what we do for a living, we exchange our time for money.

> ***"Every day is a bank account, and time is our currency. No one is rich, no one is poor, we've got 24 hours each."***
>
> ***Christopher Rice***

Knowing that time is our greatest asset, if we want to generate 10% more money, we need to manage our time in order to provide an extra 10% of it for that purpose. What this means is that if we work 40 hours per week to generate 100% of our income, we will need additional 4 hour per week to generate this additional 10%.

There are a number of jobs, in which we are paid by the hour – $10 per hour, $20 per hour, etc. In other words, our employer has agreed to pay a certain amount of money for one hour of the work we do. From our viewpoint – by working for that company, we have agreed to "sell" for that same amount of money one hour of our time. If we get a monthly salary, it is a simple calculation to find out how much our hourly wage is: we just have to divide the salary by the total working hours per month.

Why is it important for us to know the money equivalent of 1-hour work? Because it will help us to make informed decisions when choosing between different options about the optimal usage of our time. For example, we decide to start a side-project, by which we plan to make an extra 2000 $. Here comes the question: how much time will we need to invest in it? Say we earn $20 per hour from our full-time job. If the side work requires 100 hours, it means that we have managed to find a project that is *just as good* as our other job, with view to the money compensation for our time. Logically, if it requires less than 100 hours, it is more time-efficient, and if it requires more than 100 hours – less time-efficient than our full-time job. Of course, there is a limit to the number of hours one can work per day and we shall come back to the subject when discussing the life-work balance.

Knowing this we need to ask ourselves:
- Do we use our time the best way?
- Can we improve our time management?
- How having more time will help us reaching our goal?

2. Improving our time management

*"This is the key to time management –
to see the value of every moment."*

Menachem Mendel Schneerson

If we reach to the conclusion that we can be more effective in managing our time, we could use a methodology similar to the regular problem-solving and decision-making processes. There are three stages to improving our time management:
- Identifying problems;
- Implementing changes;
- Reviewing results.

Later in the book when we make our first budget we will see that the processes of time and money management are very much alike.

The first thing we need to do is to identify the problems related to the way we manage our time.

Being aware of how we spend our time is the first step in improving our time management. In order to analyze our schedule, we should keep an activity log or a diary for a week, taking notes of everything we do - with start and finish times.

After we have collected this data, we need to set aside some time to review our activities and reflect on how effectively we manage our time on a weekly basis. We have to examine carefully what are the things that slow us down, keep us from being productive or ruin our work-life balance.

3. The work-life balance

When we speak about personal time management we often refer to work-life balance.

> *"Life is all about balance. My work is very important to me, but so are my relationships. I make time for that aspect of my life, and it makes me happy having balance in my life."*
>
> ***Samantha Barks***

It is a well-known fact that not everything in this world is work and money. We need to find the balance. One way to do this is by using the "wheel of life". Here is how it works:

The wheel usually represents 8 (can vary from 6 to 9) aspects of our life competing for our time and attention.

The outside circle represents the highest level of satisfaction, while the center of the wheel represents the state of being totally dissatisfied.

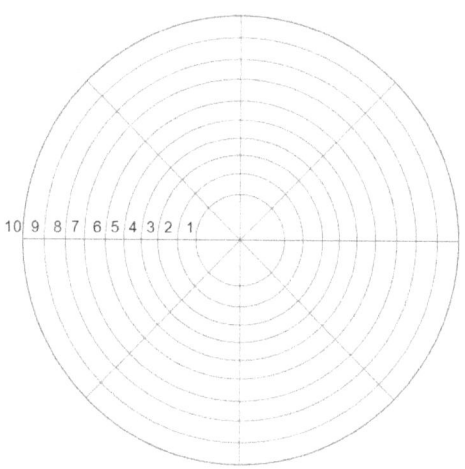

Next, we have to select the 8 most important things in our life and put them in the 8 sectors of the wheel. Certainly, these priorities vary from person to person. Here is a list with examples:
- Money;
- Health;
- Fun and Recreation;
- Hobbies;
- Significant other/Romance;

- Family;
- Friends;
- Career;
- Business;
- Work;
- Personal Growth;
- Knowledge/Intellectual;
- Spiritual/Religion;
- Personal Development;
- Physical Wellbeing;
- Emotional/Relationships;
- Environment/Community.

Once we select the 8 most important things for us, the next step is to complete the assessment. Each sector can get a score between 0 and 10 where 10 (at the outside circle), stands for the highest satisfaction possible and 0 (at the center of the wheel) – for total dissatisfaction. We need to determine our level of satisfaction for each of the 8 sectors on our "Wheel of Life" and fill it up.

Once ready, we will have something like that:

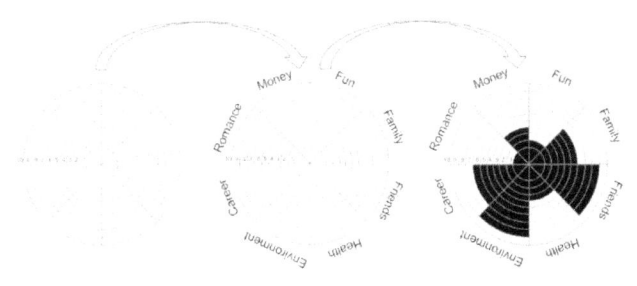

Now we have our wheel of life. Does it look balanced? What would a ride on this wheel feel like?

It is important to know that in order for us to live a balanced and satisfying life, we must have as big and round wheel as possible. From physics we know that the bigger, rounder and more balanced our wheel is, the less energy it requires to move. This way we will have more energy available to invest in other things.

> *"I don't think I'll ever feel perfectly balanced, but I feel like I'm figuring it out, and I'm surrounded by really wonderful people that want to see me succeed and be happy. Life is wild. "*
>
> *Sharon Van Etten*

What is the whole idea of this wheel and how is it connected with our personal time management? Unfortunately, when trying to find time for building wealth we usually tend to ignore something else, which is also important for us. This should never be the case. So what are our options then?

The entire idea of time management is to help us make time for our priorities, eliminating the things that waste our time.

Now we must create a weekly schedule and analyze what the time wasters are. Please remember: in this example we try to free up four hours for improving our finance. The same thing can be done for any of the 8 sectors on our wheel of life that is currently suffering due to lack of time efficiency.

4. Time wasters

> *"I am one of the great wasters of time. I have made it an art form. I can get up at 8 o'clock in the morning, be out of the house by 8:30 and back by 5 P.M., and I'll be going all day long and accomplish absolutely nothing. It's an amazing talent."*
>
> *Bob Newhart*

As already stated, it is important to track our time and create a sheet containing all our weekly activities and the time spent for each of them. This way we can determine and evaluate our time wasters.

However different the time wasters may be, most of them make us pay for someone else's profit:

- Watching TV;
- Watching sports;
- Working overtime;
- Spending time on social media.

Watching TV

"I remember when I was young, I was watching TV, and my father came into the room, agitated, and told me to start a business. I was eight years old."

Sebastian Maniscalco

This is one of the most common things that waste our time. For all the commercials that we watch we pay with our time, not getting anything in return. The advertisers promote their products and the television studios are getting paid by them to sell our time.

Nowadays we can see that, thanks to modern technology, the new generation is not as interested in watching TV shows as the ones before and therefore spends less time on it. Of course, that does not automatically mean their time management is better, as many of today's young people just replace one time waster (TV) with another (social media).

Watching sports

"I'm not going to waste time or energy spent on something I cannot control."

Eric Weddle

This is another thing that wastes our time. In order to control the masses, one has to give them a spectacle - this has been a well-known concept since Ancient Rome. That is how the phrase "panem et circenses" (bread and circuses) was born. Watching someone else play is a total waste of time. We cannot do anything to affect the final result and we pay with our time for the salary of the players. Sport is a very popular method to entertain the public. People love to support their favorite team. But let's be honest to ourselves, no matter what we do we won't change the outcome of any sport event. If we are so interested in the outcome of a game, we can just watch the highlights on the next day and invest these hours in something much more important for us.

Working overtime

"I am definitely going to take a course on time management... just as soon as I can work it into my schedule."

Louis E. Boone

Although there are rare cases when we need to do overtime at work, on most occasions this is just a symptom that we cannot manage our time. It is important to understand that working overtime could be avoided, if we learn how to be more effective. The problem here is that we usually try to fix everything ourselves, we do not prioritize or we just cannot say "no" to people.

Working overtime is very negative for our work-life balance. This problem can be easily fixed, if we start a daily journal where we put down all the tasks we have and prioritize them correctly. Also, we have to get the best of our working rhythm. It is scientifically proven that some people are more active in the mornings and others feel more creative at night. Knowing which of these groups we belong to, we can determine the optimal time to do the most complicated and important tasks, as well as that for the easy and routine ones.

Spending time on social media

"I completely understand social media as a method of promotion and digesting information, but it just seems like a colossal waste of time to me, and there's a million other ways I'd rather waste my time."

Jason Mantzoukas

The top reason of wasting time nowadays. It is addictive because we want to be liked and loved by others. This is generating happiness in our subconscious and we get addicted to the social media before we know it. Let's be honest, seeing what someone else is having for dinner or 200 pictures of a cat won't compensate the time we can spend on developing our skills and competencies.

Of course, we cannot isolate ourselves from the world, but we should definitely limit the time spent on unimportant things.

Here is a list of what we recommend instead:
- Time with our family, friends and loved ones;
- Time spend for our health and well-being;
- Time to develop and educate ourselves;

- Time for building our wealth and improving our financial status.

Below is a sample schedule that we are going to analyze:

		Monday	Tuesday	Wednesday	Thursday	Friday	Saturday	Sunday
07:00	08:00	Prepare for work	Prepare for work	Prepare for work	Prepare for work	Prepare for work	Sleep	Sleep
08:00	09:00	Travel to work	Travel to work	Travel to work	Travel to work	Travel to work	Sleep	Sleep
09:00	10:00	Work	Work	Work	Work	Work	Family time	Family time
10:00	11:00	Work	Work	Work	Work	Work	Family time	Family time
11:00	12:00	Work	Work	Work	Work	Work	Family time	Family time
12:00	13:00	Work	Work	Work	Work	Work	Family time	Meeting friends
13:00	14:00	Work	Work	Work	Work	Work	Family time	Meeting friends
14:00	15:00	Work	Work	Work	Work	Work	Family time	Meeting friends
15:00	16:00	Work	Work	Work	Work	Work	TV/Sports	TV/Sports
16:00	17:00	Work	Work	Work	Work	Work	TV/Sports	TV/Sports
17:00	18:00	Work	Work	Work	Work	Work	TV/Sports	TV/Sports
18:00	19:00	Travel to home	Overtime	Travel to home	Overtime	Overtime	Dinner	Dinner
19:00	20:00	Gym	Overtime	Gym	Overtime	Travel to home	TV	TV
20:00	21:00	Dinner	Travel to home	Dinner	Travel to home	Dinner	TV	TV
21:00	22:00	TV	Dinner	TV	Dinner	TV	Internet/Social media	Internet/Social media
22:00	23:00	Internet/Social media	Internet/Social media	Internet/Social media	Internet/Social media	Internet/Social media	Internet/Social media	Internet/Social media
23:00	07:00	Sleep	Sleep	Sleep	Sleep	Sleep	Sleep	Sleep

From the schedule it is easy to see that in this case we have wasted:
- 7 hours watching TV;
- 6 hours watching sports;

- 9 hours in social media;
- 5 hours for working overtime.

We wanted to find only 4 additional hours per week for our financial project. However, using the example above, we have identified no less than 27 hours of time wasting on a weekly basis.

For the first three items we just need to go through the change management process and motivate ourselves to stop wasting so much time. Why not read a book instead of watching TV? It is a well-known fact that really rich people normally read at least one book a week.

The last item from the list, related to the overtime hours, although a bit harder, is not impossible to deal with.

We have listed below some of the most common time management problems:

- Struggling at particular times of the day;
- Too many distractions;
- Missing deadlines;
- Procrastination;
- Waste too much time on meetings;
- Unable to say "no";
- Cannot delegate;
- Cannot prioritize.

Struggling at particular times of the day

"Rhythm is something you either have or don't have, but when you have it, you have it all over."

Elvis Presley

The main reason for this is that we are not fully aware of our working rhythm. As we mentioned earlier, some people may work better in the morning, others in the afternoon. When we make our daily schedule we will accomplish a lot more tasks, if we tackle the most important ones during our most productive part of the day.

As we are trying to win the money making game, we should focus mainly on improving after our finances. This means that if we are morning persons, it will be best to take care of our daily financial tasks first thing in the morning.

Too many distractions

"Successful people maintain a positive focus in life no matter what is going on around them. They stay focused on their past successes rather than their

past failures, and on the next action steps they need to take to get them closer to the fulfillment of their goals rather than all the other distractions that life presents to them."

Jack Canfield

If we want to stay focused and get the job done, we must minimize the potential interruptions. The modern world is full of tools to help us communicate effectively with others (e.g. phone, email, instant messaging apps etc.). While these tools can often be extremely useful, they can also prove quite distracting, particularly if our task requires high level of concentration.

In order to minimize distractions and interruptions, we could try the following: If possible, turn off email notifications and just check the inbox every couple of hours. We could even use our email's out of office assistant to reply to incoming messages, stating that we will respond when available. Also we can switch off instant messenger services. Anyone who is trying to contact us can send an email or give us a call instead.

Missing deadlines

"I love deadlines. I like the whooshing sound they make as they fly by."

Douglas Adams

If this is the reason we fail at time management, we may want to start prioritizing our daily tasks and create to-do lists. Some people have many lists – for example, they can have a separate one for each of their projects, while others prefer to have a single list containing all their daily activities. Such a list could be created either early in the morning or the evening before.

Depending on how we like to work, we could make our 'to do' lists using pen and paper, a spreadsheet, or one of the many free tools available online.

The last stage is to review our results.

It is important to reflect on how things were before we addressed our time management problems and how they are now. We should take note of the changes we can see happening and the benefits associated with each improvement we make.

In the beginning, it is recommended to dedicate at least 1 hour a day to our finances.

Procrastination

"Procrastination is the thief of time."

Edward Young

Procrastination is a common threat to personal productivity. At some point in life everyone have fallen victim to procrastination. It may affect anything from a small task to an important project at work. People procrastinate due to a number of reasons, such as:
- Lack of confidence;
- Complex nature of the task;
- Lack of interest;
- Cannot focus.

All these causes of procrastination indicate that most of the time we are on autopilot and our subconscious mind controls us. When that happens the left hemisphere of our brain (the logical one) dominates. In this state of mind, in order to keep us in our comfort zone, our brain wants to protect us by selecting the easiest option available, which in turn leads to procrastination. We need to oppose it by actively thinking and getting our brain to start being creative again. When we manage to do that, we will be able to handle every task much faster.

To master this skill, we should constantly practice. Once we learn how our brain works, we will become much more productive.

Waste too much time on meetings

"People who enjoy meetings should not be in charge of anything."

Thomas Sowell

Meetings take up enormous amount of time (and money). We should always avoid attending meetings where we are not really required – we can always get a briefing from another attendee, if necessary.
There are some basic rules to follow when it comes to meetings. First, we have to set the agenda, time frame and location of the meeting. Next, we must make sure that only the right people attend the meeting. The other important thing is to send out the agenda upfront, so that everyone can get familiar with the topics that need to be discussed. Last but not least, in order to have productive meetings, we should acquire basic facilitating skills. Doing all these things will reduce significantly the time we spend in meetings on daily basis.

Unable to say no

"We have to establish time boundaries and learn how to say no."

Alexandra Stoddard

Most of us have an innate desire to please, which can often make us say "yes" when we would rather say "no". Although a positive 'can-do' approach seems to be the best way of getting ahead in life, saying "yes" all the time can have a negative impact on work and health. It's good to help others but we are not supposed to do everything people ask of us, particularly when we risk losing focus on our own tasks. We must be assertive and turn down additional work, if we cannot handle it. It may sometimes be hard to say an outright 'no' though. So if we have trouble with this, we should try saying 'not just now' instead, and offer an alternative time when we will be available to take on these tasks.

We find ourselves in such situations because we believe that saying "no" means that we will be seen as unhelpful or selfish. There must have been times when we asked someone for something, only to be kindly told to wait because they were busy at the moment. Were we offended when this happened or did we fully understand that the other person had his/her own responsibilities and priorities? We need to turn this around and apply it to ourselves.

Another important thing is to learn to be firm and never use "maybe", as it is often misinterpreted as a potential "yes", which can unfairly raise expectations – the requester will be disappointed and will think badly of us when we eventually turn him/her down.

Cannot delegate

> *"One of the great advantages that I had in my career is I started trading 24 hours a day in my early 20s, and I had to learn to delegate to people."*
>
> *Kenneth C. Griffin*

Don't be scared of handing over work to others. When we are feeling overwhelmed, we should clarify our priorities and work out what we can realistically consign to others. As a matter of fact, if everyone in the team focuses on what they do best, the end result will be much better. There are many reasons why we might want to delegate work to people in our team. To do it successfully, we have to consider the activities that we carry out regularly and identify those that don't require our individual set of skills or our level of authority. Then we can choose the most appropriate person to delegate to, and brief him or her about the work and its timescales.

Cannot prioritize

> *"I just work hard and do things as they come along. But it has been a challenge to learn that I have to say 'no' to things and to know how and what to prioritize."*
>
> *Hanneli Mustaparta*

To be able to prioritize is one very important skill that we need to learn in our life. In the context of time management we can follow these steps to improve our way of handling tasks:
- Create a to-do list;
- Label each task on our list depending on its importance;
- Prioritize the plan.

Whether we use a specific prioritization technique or simply put down our tasks and try to complete them one by one, prioritization helps us focus on what is important. When we receive a new task, we need to priorities it against our existing workload and incorporate it into our plans accordingly. If we're using a 'to do' list, we must keep a note of the due date for each job. We may also want to set multiple deadlines for complex jobs. If we find ourselves with conflicting priorities that seem to be equally important, we should speak to our boss or colleagues and agree which one of them to address first.

Create a to-do list

> *"My to-do list is so long that it doesn't have an end; it has an event horizon."*
>
> *Craig Bruce*

It is quite easy to create a to-do list of all the tasks and activities that we need to complete. The list does not have to be in any particular order.

The most important tip when it comes to to-do lists: Our short-term memory can only hold between seven and ten items, so it can become difficult to memorize every single thing we need to do (without having it written down). Rather than getting stressed trying to remember everything, making a list will help us focus on what we have to do, as well as reduce anxiety levels.

Label each task on our list depending on its importance

> *"You need to prioritize. If you cannot get to everything or do everything, that's okay."*
>
> ***Julie Chen***

Here we can use the simple ABC method, where A's are the most important tasks, B's are those which need to be completed soon, but are not urgent and C's are the ones we can leave for the days when we are not so busy. In this method we start with the A's, continue with the B's and, if we have time, move on to the C's.

We can also use the "Eisenhower Matrix" to prioritise our tasks. This matrix has four quadrants:
- Urgent and important – these are the tasks that must be completed with

priority. Do not procrastinate these tasks;
- Urgent but not important – we must evaluate these tasks and, if we do not have enough time, delegate to someone else;
- Not urgent but important – we have to plan when we are going to complete these tasks;
- Not urgent and not important – these are the tasks that are to be eliminated from our backlog.

	Urgent	Not urgent
Important	DO	DECIDE
Not important	DELEGATE	DELETE

A third method that we can use also divides the tasks into four quadrants:
- Urgent – these tasks need to be completed first;
- Quick and easy – these tasks are to be done right after the urgent ones. Since they are easy to complete, by doing them

we will drastically reduce the task backlog;
- Plan – these are the ones that can wait or be delegated;
- Waste – the last category is the one that can be ignored and removed from the backlog.

Quick and easy	Urgent
Plan	Waste

No matter what method we decide to use, it is important to set the priority for each of our tasks.

Prioritize the plan

> *"It seems every morning I wake up to face a list of 20 things to do, with time only to do 10, and somehow I always wind up squishing in 30."*
>
> ***Karen Salmansohn***

The last step in the prioritization process is to spend several minutes of our day to create and update our to-do list. We can create it first in the morning or last thing before our working day ends. We have to make sure we update our list every time we complete a task.

5. Using time effectively

> *"What does immortality mean to me? That we all want more time; and we want it to be quality time."*
>
> **Joan D. Vinge**

Once we improve our time management, we are one step closer to reaching our goal. Since we now have several hours to spend for building wealth, we must decide how to use this time.

Different options exist, but what we would recommend is to start educating and developing ourselves:
- Read more nonfiction literature for self-development purposes;
- Read successful people's stories and biographies;

- Spend enough time with our friends and family;
- Find enough time to take good care of our health.

Read more nonfiction literature for self-development purposes

"I love books so much. I've read more books than anyone else I know."

Daniel Tammet

We have already highlighted how important reading is for our self-development. At the same time, it should be noted that the right choice of books can greatly accelerate our progress. Reading fiction develops our imagination, while reading nonfiction literature helps us obtain particular knowledge in our field of interest.

The best thing to do, once we have provided more time to read, is focus on the books that will make us better specialists by acquiring new skills and expertise. These books might not be as fun as the latest novel of our favorite author but they will certainly prove their worth in the long run. The good news? We don't have to stop reading the books we enjoy but rather add to our list the ones that will contribute to achieving the goals we set.

Read successful people's stories and biographies

"No great man lives in vain. The history of the world is but the biography of great men."

Thomas Carlyle

There are so many interesting stories of people who made their dreams come true. No matter how wealthy and famous they are now, most of them have started their journey to success just like everyone of us - having their doubts and fears, faced with tough decisions to take, being in debt, etc. We can learn a lot from their experience and mistakes, follow their advice or choose a completely different path. Some of them will inspire us, others will help us realize that we need to change but, most importantly, their stories will make us believe what we are trying to achieve is possible, if we give it our best shot.

Spend enough time with our friends and family

"We don't have the luxury of time. We spend more because of how we live, but it's important to be with our family and friends."

Sara Blakely

As already discussed, when talking about the wheel of life, our work-life balance is a key fundamental to success. Our ambition to make more money cannot be a reason for neglecting the people we love and care about. They share our joys and support us in difficult moments. If we don't have enough time for our family and friends, this is a clear sign that we should optimize and/or reorganize our activities.

Otherwise, we put ourselves at risk of burnout. It could materialize in lack of concentration, decreased productivity and high level of stress. Last but not least, we have to take under consideration the well-known fact that working more does not necessarily mean working better.

Find enough time to take good care of our health

"The first wealth is health."

Ralph Waldo Emerson

We should keep in mind that winning the money making game cannot happen overnight - it has to be our long term goal. Staying healthy and fit is a crucial prerequisite to achieving it. In this regard, we must never endanger our health to make fast cash.
No matter how busy we are, we need to remain physically active, eat quality foods and do regular medical checkups.
As it was wisely said:

"Of the five most important things in life, health is first, education or knowledge is second, and wealth is third. I forget the other two."

Chuck Berry

People often overlook their health needs and suffer the consequences of that poor decision. In truth, with just a few changes in our daily routine, we could greatly improve our health and wellness. That will have a beneficial effect on every aspect of our life.

In conclusion, we would like to reiterate that our health depends on us and we ought to do our best to protect it. If we want to be able to enjoy the riches we are about to earn, we have to take care of ourselves.

TURNING MOTIVATION INTO HABIT

"Motivation is what gets you started. Habit is what keeps you going."

Jim Ryun

What is motivation?
The short answer is that this is the urge which makes people act in a certain way.
Motivation is a great thing to have when we start something new but the main problem is that it is temporary. This is the reason why we usually fail in the long run, although we want to accomplish something and improve our life.
Of course, this negative scenario is easy to overcome, if we use the motivation momentum and work on turning it into habit. In other

words, habit will prevail over impulse in the long run.

In this chapter we will discuss how it can be done.

Motivation is the starting point of all achievements. We must not mistake it for hope or a simple wish. If we do, it will slip away from us very fast. And that is why we must make sure we do not leave a possible way of retreat.

1. Understanding personal motivation

> *"With the proper motivation, you can do anything. I was just a poor kid that ate pork and beans out of a can and apple sauce. I went from rags to riches. But it does take a lot of determination, inner strength, drive, and discipline."*
>
> ***Lee Haney***

When it comes to personal motivation, it's important to remember that different people have different drivers for motivation. Some are driven by the prospect of challenging work and the opportunity to develop their skills and expertise, while others relish the chance to take additional responsibilities.

In his 1961 book "The Achieving Society", David McClelland proposed that there are three key needs that drive people's motivation:
- The need for achievement;
- The need for affiliation;
- The need for power.

The need for achievement

> *"Happiness lies in the joy of achievement and the thrill of creative effort."*
>
> *Franklin D. Roosevelt*

These people are driven by the prospect of performing well. They want to attain or surpass set standards, make a significant contribution to the organization's aims and achieve their career goals.

The main characteristics of achievement-motivated people are:
- Meeting or surpassing standards of excellence;
- Making a significant and unique contribution;
- Competing successfully with others;
- Realizing personal goals.

The need for affiliation

"We can live without religion and meditation, but we cannot survive without human affection."

Dalai Lama

In order to feel motivated, they need to develop and maintain good relationships with others at work. Affiliation-oriented people want to feel like they belong to their team and organization and that they are accepted by others. They perform well in an environment with minimal conflict.

The main characteristics of affiliation-motivated people are:
- Being part of a group or a team;
- Being liked and accepted;
- Being involved with others;
- Minimizing the degree of conflict.

The need for power

"True happiness involves the full use of one's power and talents."

John W. Gardner

Power-oriented people are driven by the need to impress others and exert influence over people and situations. They relish responsibility and like to be in control. These individuals like to be able to carve out a reputation for themselves and they place a great deal of value on their status and position in the organization.

The main characteristics of power-motivated people are:

- Having control over situations;
- Ability to influence others;
- Recognition through status/position;
- Greater responsibility;
- Building a reputation.

Most people are motivated by a combination of these three needs, but one driver is usually dominant. Knowing our dominant will help us find out what motivates us the most. On the other hand, by knowing the three motivation types, we can easily determine other people's motivating factors. That will improve our communication skills and the way we work with others.

"Knowing others is wisdom, knowing ourselves is Enlightenment."

Lao Tzu

Our motivation dominant can change over time but it is important that, once we determine it, we start using it to our advantage. Thus, we can stay motivated over a long period of time to become rich and build our wealth.

For example, if our dominant is "achievement", we can set a healthy inner competition, in order to keep our motivation going for as long as possible. If our type is "affiliation", we can build our motivation to become wealthy by setting goals to help others. The "power" type can build their motivation around the idea that they will create the reputation and social status they want.

In 1954, psychologist Abraham Maslow suggested that motivation was linked to the satisfaction of human needs. In his book "Motivation and Personality" he presented the "Hierarchy of Human Needs", often depicted as a pyramid, which outlines five sets of needs. According to this classification, it is a certain need that dominates the human organism.

Starting from bottom to top, here are the five sets of needs:
- Physiological needs;
- Security;
- Love and belongingness;
- Esteem;
- Self-actualization.

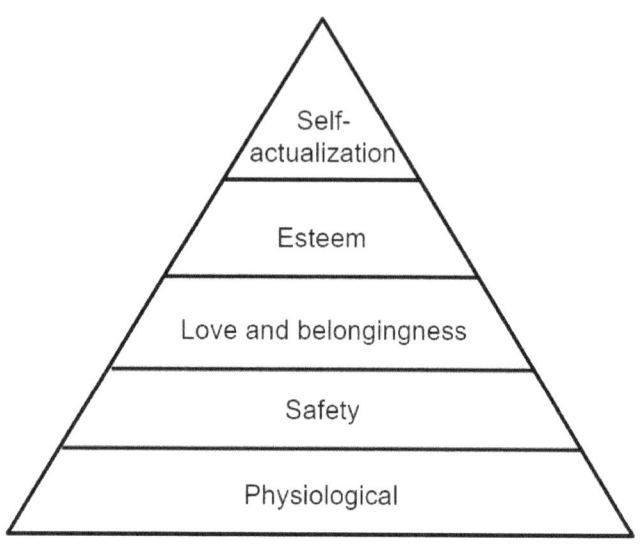

Physiological needs

"Well the real concept of basic needs if you cut it right down are simply the physical needs that are unavoidable for all of us. So to have enough calories to keep our bodies going. Have shelter from extreme elements. To have water that is safe to drink, so I think that's the core of it."

Peter Singer

These basic needs are related to the physical requirements for human survival. They are the most straightforward needs in the entire hierarchy. If the physiological needs are not met, the human body cannot function properly. Undoubtedly, they are of highest importance and therefore should be addressed first. Physiological needs include:

- Breathing;
- Water;
- Food;
- Rest;
- Sleep.

In our everyday life we do not pay special attention to these needs as they are part of our routine. Fulfilling them keeps our inner balance, while neglecting them forces our body to ignore everything else and kick into survival mode. In other words, if we fail to meet our physiological needs, it will be impossible for us to move up the pyramid to its higher four levels.

Safety needs

"At the end of the day, the goals are simple: safety and security."

Jodi Rell

Once we have satisfied our physiological needs, our safety needs become the dominant factor. There are various aspects of safety, related to:
- Home;
- Money;
- Job;
- Order;
- Healthcare.

The second level of the pyramid is as important as the first one but this time our mindset and emotions are decisive. Everyone's perception of the world is different and so are our safety needs. Nevertheless, most people prefer to be in control in every possible way and their life to be well organized.

At this stage people often associate the money they earn with a certain level of safety. This is the main reason why many of them prefer to keep their jobs and not work toward their dreams. However, there are strategies that can increase our level of security and still make us generate wealth.

After the physiological and safety needs are fulfilled, the third level of human needs is interpersonal and involves feelings of belongingness.

> *"People first concern themselves with meeting their basic needs; only afterwards, do they pursue any higher needs."*
>
> *Abdolkarim Soroush*

Again it is important that the first two levels of the pyramid are met before we can move to this stage.

Love and belongingness needs

> *"By building relations we create a source of love and personal pride and belonging that makes living in a chaotic world easier."*
>
> *Susan Lieberman*

They refer to personal relationships and include:
- Friendships;
- Intimacy;
- Family.

Once the basic needs are met, then a person can focus on their social needs. In our modern society, many people suffer because their needs of love and belonging are not met. That is why it is very important in order to build our wealth to balance our life in a way that these needs are met.

Esteem needs

> ***"Self-esteem is the reputation we acquire with ourselves."***
>
> ***Nathaniel Branden***

They are also ego needs or status needs and they develop a concern with:
- Recognition;
- Status;
- Importance;
- Respect from others.

All humans have a need to feel respected and that they play a part in the world. This includes the need to have self-esteem and self-respect. Esteem presents the typical human desire to be accepted and valued by others. We as people want to feel that we have accomplished things that are valuable and important. We want to be independent and do things for ourselves. People often engage in a profession or hobby to gain recognition that will insure them a sense of contribution.

In our modern society people with low self-esteem often need respect from others. They may feel the need to seek fame or glory. However, fame or glory will not help the person to build their self-esteem until they accept who they are internally.

There are two versions of esteem needs:

- Lower – it is usually associated with the need for respect from others. This may include a need for status, recognition, fame, prestige and attention;
- Higher – is the need for self-respect.

Self-actualization

> *"We cannot be truly happy without becoming everything that we want to become."*
>
> ***Abraham Maslow***

The last level of the pyramid is the perceived need for self-actualization. This level of need refers to what a person's full potential is and the realization of that potential. These needs do not show themselves until all of the needs in the previous levels have been taken care of. This is the level that we need to reach as end goal of our journey to wealth.

The five basic sets of needs cause us to want or desire certain things. The closer we come to satisfying one need, the more we want to satisfy the next need in the hierarchy. It is essential to understand that just because we may want something, does not mean we will try to get it.

Of course there are a lot of exceptions in this hierarchy. For example there are people for which the self-esteem is more important than love and belonging. In these cases we can observe a switch between the two levels. This is caused mostly because they think that having self-esteem makes us strong, powerful and respected. Other common exception is related to people who have lived their whole life worrying about the basic needs. The constant fear and worrying about having enough food and shelter prevent them to move to the higher levels. As a side effect they cannot build wealth and levels of self-esteem and self-actualization can disappear completely. There are many more exceptions but we are not going to cover them in this book.

This theory remains popular and continue to provide valuable insights. It is important to understand what are the different needs that drive our motivation and to know where are we currently in our journey to building wealth.

Of course there are many other theories created after this one but the basic principles remain the same.

After understanding this basic theory we need to ask ourselves:
- Why do some people go the extra mile while others seem reluctant to get into the starting blocks?
- What is it that motivates us to work hard and how can we take responsibility for our own motivation?

As already stated motivation is the driver behind satisfying needs. We all have certain basic needs to fulfil. Poor people way of thinking is often limited only to the need for food and water, the need for shelter and protection.

Once these basic needs are satisfied, personal and aspirational needs take over. One of the main purposes of this book is for us to start focusing on our emotional well-being and the need for recognition so that we can fulfil our potential and enjoy the feeling of fulfilment. This is when motivation becomes personal.

2. Motivation and money

"When people ask me what my motivation is, I have a simple answer: money."

Jerry Reed

Now is the time to make our motivation plan lasts from the beginning until reaching our goal of becoming rich. To do this we need to define exactly:

- The amount of money we want to accumulate;
- What are we willing to give in return for this amount of money;
- A date when we intend to possess the money.

We recommend that we write down clearly the amount of money, date of acquisition, what we expect to give in return and our plans. Make sure we put it somewhere that we can see it every day.

Once our plan is established we need to be persistent. The road to becoming reach it's not an easy one. Do not ever give up once we have put our decisions into action. Do not be scared. We all have hard times. The best option to face hard times is persistence. We may fail. But we have to begin chasing our dreams again. Keep in mind that 90% of all first attempts to become rich fail. But 100% is the rate of failing our goal if we do not start at all. The greatest positions remain for the people who do not know what 'give up' means.

To develop persistence we must:

- Have a definite purpose backed by motivation for its fulfillment;
- Follow the plan and take continuous actions toward accomplishing it;
- Isolate ourselves from all external negative and discouraging influences, including negative suggestions of relatives, friends and acquaintances;
- Insure that we have support and make a friendly alliance with one or more persons who will encourage one to follow through with both plan and purpose.

How to put all this into practice? In order to answer this question we will need to use all of the learned so far for change management, time management and motivation.

- Find our inner motivation to start the transformation from our current to the future state we want to be in;

- Be prepared for the internal subconscious resistance coming from the fact that we are leaving our comfort zone. Find our own meaning of the incoming change to overcome the resistance as fast as possible;
- Revise how we manage our time and make sure we have enough time planned in our day to reach our goal;
- Create a plan with all the targets such as amount, deadline, etc. we want to accomplish;
- Analyze and monitor our process;
- Be persistent on doing this daily until we embed it as a habit.

PART II: THE PRACTICAL RULES OF THE MONEY MAKING GAME

BASIC MONEY PRINCIPLES

In the first part of the book we look at how important it is to develop the right mindset to approach the game of money making. In the following chapters we move on to our next goal – to put the newly acquired knowledge in practice.

> *"You must gain control over your money or the lack of it will forever control you."*
>
> **Dave Ramsey**

What is money and how does it work? These two questions find their answers in the pages to

follow. To be able to understand and apply the basic money principles, first we have to be aware of the three main functions of money:
- A unit of account – Money determines the values of all goods and services and allows us to compare them. Let's illustrate it with the following example: One orange costs $2, one apple costs $1, therefore the orange is twice more expensive than the apple;
- A medium of exchange – Using the same example: Say we grow oranges and someone else grows apples. When we want to get apples for our oranges, we need one orange to get two apples. Fair enough, but what if we want a pineapple and our partner needs some raspberries? As we both do not grow them, the barter trade would simply not work this time. Therefore, we collect the money for our produce and choose to buy anything that equals the same amount of dollars;
- A store of value – Why is someone trying to make money? Probably because they want to be rich, i.e. to achieve a higher standard of living, consume more, invest, provide a better future for the kids, etc. All that is

perfectly in line with the third function of money – we can save it and use it later (unlike the oranges and apples – they go bad in a week or two and have to be thrown away).

1. Money essentials

Having in mind the above-said, we can move to our list of basic money principles. Although it is not a panacea, the list gives a good starting point for the wannabe money maker:
- Start saving;
- Create an emergency fund;
- Money never sleeps;
- Money will stay with us, only if we protect it.

Start saving

> *"If saving money is wrong, I don't want to be right!"*
>
> ***William Shatner***

Money comes to those who save. Make sure the first thing we do with our money every month is to save at least 10% of it.

There is a brilliant quote on the subject by **John Rampton**:

"A cardinal rule in budgeting and saving is to pay ourselves first. Once your paycheck hits your account, wisdom has it that you should move some amount to savings even before you pay the bills."

It is very important to do this at the beginning of the month, not at the end of it. One easy way to do it, is to automatically transfer 10% of our incoming money flow to a another account of ours – we can call it "savings account", although it does not have to be a monthly bank deposit or anything of that sort. It just needs to be a separate account which we do not use for our everyday payments.

Create an emergency fund

"Do you have an emergency fund? If not, build one – aim for three months of expenses to start, then boost it to six. It will ease your anxiety and get you out of a potential jam."

Jean Chatzky

As explained in the Change Management Chapter, life offers a number of unexpected, even impossible to predict, situations. What we can do, though, to prepare ourselves for them is to create an emergency fund. It is a form of saving, but with a different purpose – to cover expenses that were not planned in advance. For that reason, the money for emergency must be easier to access. In order not to mix our primary savings with the allocations for our emergency fund, do not store them at the same place or in the same account.

Our financial discipline will be tested by the emergency fund in two ways – first, to accumulate it, instead of spending the money, and second, once we have it, to use it only when absolutely necessary. As suggested by the quote above, the optimal-in-size emergency fund should be able to cover our regular expenses for a period between 3 and 6 months.

Money never sleeps

> *"It's not how much money you make, but how much money you keep, how hard it works for you, and how many generations you keep it for."*
>
> *Robert Kiyosaki*

Only saving without the right investment won't get us to our final goal of getting rich and wealthy. Money never gets tired and can work for us 24/7.

In the following chapters we will go into detail on the economic logic of investing and on how to build a successful investment strategy. Here we would just mention that the major difference between saving and investing is the level of risk, related to each of them. While savings are considered to be almost risk-free, the more profitable the potential investments look, the riskier they get.

Money will stay with us only if we protect it

"Even though I'm already successful and have a career, it is always good to have your eggs in more than one basket."

Farrah Abraham

Same principle applies for our investment. If we invest all our money in only one thing, we risk losing it completely. Having more than one source of income, investing in more than one venture, making a "Plan B" is what rich people do.

Of course, to have our money well protected does not boil down to only making good financial decisions. It requires taking measures to physically defend our wealth from thieves, fraud, unfair practices, scams, etc.

Having all that in mind, we have selected some pieces of advice on how to handle our money better:

- Trust only people who know how to make money;
- Never invest in something we do not have any idea of;
- Make realistic expectations when setting our goals for building wealth;
- Think twice before investing;
- Don't listen to everybody;
- Creating wealth is simple and it is all around us;
- We need to be able to control our emotions;
- Opportunities come and go.

Trust only people who know how to make money

I will tell you the secret to getting rich on Wall Street. You try to

> *be greedy when others are fearful. And you try to be fearful when others are greedy.*
>
> *Warren Buffett*

We have chosen this popular quote to highlight that we should follow the guidance of the ones who have already succeeded in what we are trying to accomplish. They are today what you aim to be tomorrow, that is why we could benefit from learning how they have managed to do it. Their way of thinking and the way they acted in the key moments of their lives could serve us as a reference point. Also, we can use the mistakes that they have made as lessons learned.

Never invest in something we do not have any idea of

> *"It amazes me how people are often more willing to act based on little or no data than to use data that is a challenge to assemble."*
>
> *Robert Shiller*

If we want to make good investment, we should gather and analyze as much information as possible, ask questions, educate ourselves. We should be a critical thinker, always double-check our sources and make sure we know exactly what we are doing. We should be also aware what is at stake – calculate the potential profit, but the potential loss as well. The fact that something has worked fine for someone else is not a guarantee that it would work for us too. Last but not least, remember that investing is not gambling.

Make realistic expectations when setting our goals for building wealth

"Money is multiplied in practical value depending on the number of W's you control in your life: what you do, when you do it, where you do it, and with whom you do it."

Tim Ferriss

Let us stress once again that building wealth is a journey – to reach the end of it, we must possess one virtue that we highly value: common sense. If we want to become a millionaire overnight, we will only experience disappointment and loss of motivation. On the other hand, if we are systematic and achieve many small goals one by one, eventually we will become rich. Again, it is about having the answers to most questions in advance, rather than praying for a miracle with our eyes closed.

Think twice before investing

> *"Investing isn't about beating others at their game. It's about controlling ourselves at our own game."*
>
> *Benjamin Graham*

Above all, when we decide to invest money, we turn down a lot of other ways to use it. This is not a bad thing, but rather – a matter of choice. To feel confident that we are making the right one, we should find the answers to the following questions:
- Is this the best thing I can do with my money?
- Can I afford it?
- Is this the right time?
- What is the time frame of the investment – short-term, mid-term,

long-term? (Do I have the patience to wait for the positive outcome?)
- Do I have an exit strategy from the investment?

Keep reading and we hope that pretty soon we will be able to win the money making game.

Don't listen to everybody around us

> *"You can listen to what everybody says, but the fact remains that we've got to get out there and do the thing ourselves."*
>
> *Joan Sutherland*

This message is crystal clear. We have already touched upon the subject in the previous chapters – there is no way and no need to get everyone's approval. It is even worse to let others be in control of our actions. He who listens to everybody will only become a laughing stock. All our decisions must be based on our own expertise, motivation and experience.

Creating wealth is simple and it is all around us

"What's keeping you from being rich? In most cases it's simply a lack of belief. In order to become rich, you must believe you can do it, and you must take the actions necessary to achieve your goal."

Suze Orman

What we mean is that if we are determined to become rich, stop dreaming about it and start acting accordingly. Even the best idea will remain only an idea, if not put into practice. When we see the potential in something that we are capable of doing – forget about the excuses and do it or someone else will. It is really as simple as that.

We are convinced that if we read 100 success stories and biographies of rich people, we would almost instinctively think: "That doesn't seem complicated at all. I could have done it even better." And, interestingly enough, we would be right.

We need to be able to control our emotions

"In the world of money and investing, you must learn to control your emotions."

Robert Kiyosaki

In general, no matter what our occupation us, if we lose our temper, it is more likely that the end result will be worse. In contrast, keeping a cool head will help us solve a lot of difficult problems and will prevent us from making many silly mistakes.

Have in mind that love, hate, happiness or sadness have nothing to do with money making. It is about rational choices, profit maximization, cost-benefit analysis, investment portfolio optimization, etc. In short, we have to get the numbers right.

As we are all humans, our emotions quite interfere with our rational thinking. The best thing to do – try to lower as much as possible the level of stress in our life.

Opportunities come and go

"Opportunity is missed by most people because it is dressed in overalls and looks like work."

Thomas Edison

Being able to know when to make quick decisions is an important skill. We often fail to recognize it and keep complaining that life hasn't given us the chance to become successful. It is important to evaluate every opportunity and take the ones that (according to our calculations and forecasts) will lead us to a wealthy life.

The main cause of poverty or financial struggle is fear and ignorance, not the economy or the government. So when the next chance appears, make it count. We will always be rewarded for the continued effort and perseverance we show, when others quit.

2. Personal financial statements

"Assets put money in your pocket, whether you work or not, and liabilities take money from your pocket."

Robert Kiyosaki

Have we ever looked at our bank statements and got surprised that we had spent more than we thought? Well, to be honest we all did at some point. When that happens we need to take measures not to get in such a situation anymore.

There is a simple method of accounting for income and expenses that can help us avoid overspending – create our personal financial statements. Being similar to the ones used by corporations, they will provide us with an indication of our financial condition and can help with budget planning. When speaking about personal financial statements, we usually refer to one of the following :

- The personal money flow statement;
- The personal balance sheet.

The personal money flow statement measures our money inflows and outflows and, based on them, determines the net money flow.

Money inflows

> *"Never take your eyes off the cash flow because it's the life blood of business."*
>
> *Richard Branson*

They are literally anything that brings in money and include the following:
- Salaries;
- Interest from savings accounts;
- Dividends from investments;
- Financial gains from stocks and bonds;
- Income from properties, etc.

Money outflows

> ***"The three most dreaded words in the English language are 'negative cash flow'."***
>
> ***David Tang***

On the other hand, they represent all expenses, regardless of size, and may include:
- Rent;
- Mortgage payments;
- Utility bills;
- Groceries;
- Taxes;
- Spending on books, movies, tickets, restaurants, etc.

We suggest that we take a close look at our money inflows and outflows. Most likely we will find out that we belong to one of the following four groups:

- Relatively constant inflows and outflows – This is the most common pattern. An example for it: A person working on a salary, paying rent and/or a bank loan with a fixed monthly installment. It is the easiest and safest option, as far as financial planning is concerned. On the other hand, it could make us stay within our comfort zone for too long, thus refusing to take risks and accept challenges;
- Relatively constant inflows and variable outflows – If we bring in similar amounts of money each month, but our expenses are different, that shows a risky spending behavior. It can be seen quite often nowadays, as once in a while people tend to buy fancy things they could not afford. If not addressed early enough, such irregularity will get us into debt;
- Variable inflows and relatively constant outflows – In this scenario, we switch between different jobs, projects or business activities, while our expenses remain the same. This option is also riskier than the first one, but it has a

bigger potential – being more flexible and open to new opportunities may bring us a higher income;
- Variable inflows and outflows – This is definitely the worst pattern of all. It shows that we are not able to control and predict neither our income, nor our expenses. Of course, that makes us feel insecure and stresses us out. If we happen to find ourselves in such a situation, we should try to get out of it as fast as we can.

Let us point out that in different periods of time we could move back and forth between the 4 scenarios described above (our inflows and outflows may change). That is something we don't have to worry about, as long as we monitor the process and take corrective measures when needed.

Along with analyzing the dynamics of our money inflows and outflows, we have to calculate the net money flow. It gives us the general picture of how good or bad we are doing at the moment.

Net money flow

"Entrepreneurs believe that profit is what matters most in a new enterprise. But profit is secondary.

Cash flow matters most."

Peter Drucker

Our net money flow is the result of subtracting our outflow from our inflow. A positive net money flow means that we have earned more than we have spent and that you have some money left. A negative net money flow shows that we have spent more money than we have brought in. A balanced net money flow suggests that our total income equals our total spending.

To do the calculation right, make sure that the time frame of the money inflow is the same as the one of the outflow – week, month, year, etc.

Balance sheet

The second financial statement is the balance sheet. It provides an overall snapshot of our wealth at a specific moment in time. It is a summary of our:
- Assets (what we own);
- Liabilities (what we owe);
- Net worth (assets minus liabilities).

Assets

Our personal assets can be classified into the following categories:
- Liquid Assets – things we own that can easily be sold or turned into cash without losing value. These include:
  - Checking accounts;
  - Money market accounts;
  - Savings accounts;
  - Certificates of deposit (CDs);
  - Cash.
- Large Assets – they include:
  - Houses;
  - Cars;
  - Artwork;
  - Furniture.
- Investments – they include:
  - Bonds;
  - Stocks;
  - CDs (can be categorized here as well as in liquid assets);
  - Mutual funds;
  - Real estate.

Liabilities

Liabilities are what we owe and include:
- Bills;

- Payments for cars and houses;
- Credit card balances;
- Loans.

Net worth

The net worth is the difference between what we own and what we owe. This figure is our measure of wealth because it represents what we own after everything we owe has been paid off.

Logically, there are two ways to increase our net worth:
- Increase our assets;
- Decrease our liabilities.

Growing our net worth through an asset increase will only work if it is greater than the increase in liabilities. Analogically, a decrease in what we owe has to be greater than the reduction in our assets.

Keeping close track of our net money flow can actually help us in our quest to increase our net worth.

As we mentioned above, depending on our current financial situation, our net money flow could be negative, balanced or positive. No matter what it is right now, there is always room for improvement. One way to achieve it is to analyze our spending and adjust them as necessary. Another way is to find a new income source while keeping the spending at the same level. The ideal scenario is to combine the spending adjustment with a new income. If we manage to do so, the positive effect on our net money flow will be maximized. By using personal financial statements to become more aware of our spending habits and net worth, we will be well on our way to greater financial security. This is important for us to understand, as in the next chapter we will start with planning our personal budget.

3. Interest – the "price" of money

> ***"Profits in business always depend on the rate of interest: the higher the interest, the higher the rate of profit required."***
>
> ***James Buchan***

Everyone knows by heart the price of what he or she usually buys from the store. A bottle of milk or a cup of coffee costs a certain amount of money. But have we asked ourselves what is the price of money itself? Could money have a lot of different prices within the same country?

The answer to these questions is – the interest rate.

It is a fundamental principle in economics that:
"One dollar today costs more than one dollar tomorrow".

Why is that? Because nobody can be 100% sure what the future might bring, as uncertainty and risk always play part in the story. Therefore, if we decide to do something with our money in three months or in three years' time (instead of today), the results could be completely different.

Say we give somebody $1000 as a three-month loan. Technically, they are blocked for us – we lose the opportunity to use them in any possible way for that period of time – spend, invest, even gamble. By lending the money, we automatically start carrying at least two different risks:

- The money not to be returned;
- The money to lose some of its value by the time of return.

What if we do the same exercise for a period of three years? Imagine how much greater those risks (and missed opportunities) would be. Taking all that into account, economists have introduced the interest rate. We dare say it is the "price" of money, because through it we can quite accurately determine how much it would cost to use somebody else's financial resources (if we are the borrower) or how much our reward should be for not using our money (if we are the lender). The time factor is of the utmost importance: the longer the period – the higher the price of money, i.e. the interest rate. In the example above, it would be twelve times more expensive to get a three-year loan compared to a three-month one.

What about the banks – are they lenders or borrowers of money? Certainly, they could be both at the same time, but most of all they are intermediaries. They make their profit by the margin between two different prices of the same amount of money. How is that possible? Say we make a one-year bank deposit of $1000. By giving our money to the bank we do two things at once:

- We invest the $1000 almost risk-free and get a reward for that (for example 1%);
- We lend $1000 to the bank, so that it can use it for 1 year.

Somebody else goes to the bank and takes a one-year credit of $1000. The bank charges him 5% for that and gives him our $1000. The final result: the bank pockets the margin between 5% and 1% equals 4%. It "bought" our

$1000 for 1% interest and "sold" it for 5% interest, thus making a good profit.

The figure below gives a good overview of the whole process:

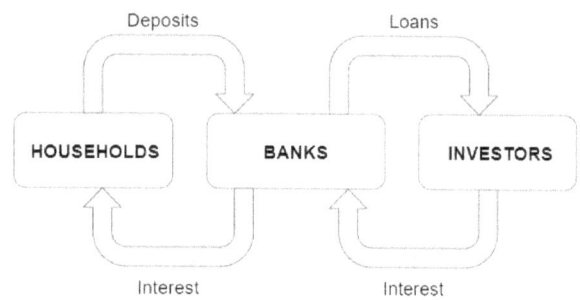

One last point – to always know the real price of our money, we should take into consideration the inflation (or deflation) rate. Generally, it shows whether our money can buy the same things or not after a given time period. If the inflation is 0%, then there is no change. If the inflation is 1%, then we can buy 1% less with our money. If there is a deflation of minus 1%, then we can buy 1% more than before.

Coming back to our example – for the one-year period of our bank deposit we received 1% interest, while the inflation for the period was also 1%. The net result for us is zero, so we ended up with the same amount of money in real terms. Our decision to put the money in the bank protected it from inflation. That way we didn't make money, but also we didn't lose money (if we had simply saved $1000 and had stored them in our house, we would have lost 1% due to inflation).

The following figure illustrates the difference between the real and the nominal interest rate:

Nominal vs Real Interest Rate

9% = 4% + 5%

Nominal Interest Rate = Real Interest Rate + Inflation Premium

In conclusion we can say that the interest rate we get for our money is their nominal price for a given period of time. When we adjust it with the inflation rate, we get their real price for that period.

Interest rates are involved on daily basis in numerous cases of lending and borrowing money. In general, people take bank credits to:
- Purchase real estate – a house, an apartment, a plot of land;

- Buy a car;
- Buy electronics, household good, furniture, finance repair works;
- Fund personal projects – education, special training;
- Start own businesses;
- Cover unexpected expenses – related to health issues, damaged property, etc.

Businesses, on the other hand, also take loans, but for different purposes such as:

- To fund capital projects;
- To expand the scope of their operations by purchasing fixed and long-term assets such as land, buildings, machinery, trucks, etc.

With lending a large asset, the lender (in most of the cases – a bank) may have been able to generate income from the asset.

Either way, the difference between the total repayment sum and the original loan is the interest charged, i.e. the interest rate applied on the principal amount.

To help us understand the interest rate concept better, we shall explain what is a simple and what is a compound interest rate.

Simple interest rate is a quick and easy method of calculating the interest amount, charged on a loan. It is applied to the original principal only. For example, if we take a $1000 loan and we are supposed to pay it back, being charged 5% simple interest, then the final amount due will be $1050. It usually applies to short-term personal loans and therefore it is not very common to see such interest rate very often.

The compound interest rate is a more complicated one. That is because it takes into account the time value of money, which was briefly explained above. Compound interest can be thought of as "interest on interest", because for each period after the first one, it is not only the principal being charged with the interest, but the new amount, including both the principal and the accumulated interest so far. Certainly, compound interest will make the amount due quite bigger, compared to the one charged with simple interest.

Compound interest is calculated, using the following formula:

$$A = P(1 + \frac{r}{n})^{nt}$$

Where:

A = the future value of the investment/loan, including interest

P = the principal investment amount (the initial deposit or loan amount)

r = the annual interest rate (decimal)

n = the number of times that interest is compounded per year

nt = the number of years the money is invested or borrowed for

Note that this formula gives us the future value of an investment or loan, which is compound interest plus the principal. Should we wish to calculate the compound interest only, we need this:

Total compounded interest:

$$P(1 + \frac{r}{n})^{nt} - P$$

Let us highlight once again that compound interest takes into consideration the accumulated interest from previous periods, thus the interest amount itself is not the same for all periods (unlike the case of the simple interest). When calculating compound interest, the number of compounding periods makes a significant difference – the higher the number of compounding periods, the greater the amount of compound interest. Being well aware of the time value of money and the exponential growth, created by compounding, is vital for optimizing our personal finances.

Compounding can work against us if we have revolving loans that carry very high interest rates, such as credit cards. They allow us to re-use the money within our credit limit, but if we are not able to pay back what we have spent during the same period, the compound interest rule applies and we start paying interest over the already-high interest plus principal.

Knowing this, if we have the ambition to gain wealth, we will need to change our way of thinking: be a lender, not a borrower.

Understanding how money works is an essential rule in the money making game. Making our money work for us always starts with creating a budget and this is what the next chapter is all about. Later in the book, there are shown several methods of handling our debt, so that we are no longer a borrower and ways to start generating extra income, in order to become a lender.

MAKING THE FIRST BUDGET

"Don't tell me what you value, show me your budget, and I'll tell you what you value."

Joe Biden

The first and most important thing we need, as we learn the rules of money making, is a personal budget. Some of us might have one, some might not. Either way, making a written budget and keeping track of it is a must. It may sound easy to do, but most people fail on this first step. This is mainly because they want to become millionaires overnight. A simple fact is that in order to achieve something significant in life, we ought to put a great effort into it.
"Rome was not built in a day."

We have probably heard this wise saying on a number of occasions. But have we tried to actually benefit from it?

Yes, it is so tempting to scratch a lottery ticket and forget about all our daily concerns on the spot. But let's be honest now – how many lottery millionaires do we personally know? We bet the answer would gravitate around zero. Let's refer to another quote:

"There's no free lunch."

Makes sense, right? Somebody somehow has to pay for it. It is common to ask a poor person how much money they have spent last year on clothes or food and they wouldn't know. On the other hand, a wealthy individual would relative easy give us quite a good answer. Why is that? Because they know how hard it is to make money and how easy – to lose it.

If we are currently living from paycheck to paycheck, perhaps it is because with every increase of our income, we raise our spendings as well. Our observations show that the vast majority of people is looking to earn more but not so many of them think how to spend the money right.

"Look at our society. Everyone wants to be thin, but nobody wants to diet.

Everyone wants to live long, but few will exercise. Everybody wants money, yet seldom will anyone budget or control their spending."

John C. Maxwell

We could be happy, even with very little in our lives, but the minute we are given something bigger and better, we want even more. We lose our sleep, our happiness, we hurt the people around us – a high price to pay for our growing needs and desires. We must learn to maintain a balance between our needs and desires, in order to enjoy a happy life with what we already have.

1. What is a budget?

"It's clearly a budget. It's got a lot of numbers in it."

George W. Bush

A budget is a financial plan for a given period of time – a month, a year, etc. It has two opposite sides – a positive and a negative one. The positive side includes all the money we take in for that time frame, and the negative side – all the money we spend during the same period. It is a statement of the amounts of money we allocate to different items, goods, services or activities that we will undertake. In our personal budget we decide how to divide our financial resources between them, so that we have enough money to cover each expense. All in all, the budgeting process is a method of planning and controlling our activities in line with our financial objectives.

> *"A budget tells us what we cannot afford, but it doesn't keep us from buying it."*
>
> ***William Feather***

There are four main stages that we go through when we create and use a budget:
- Set a budget goal – This is where we decide what we want to achieve by creating the budget;
- Decide on the type and the complexity of our budget – There are many different types of budget and they vary in purpose, content and format, depending on our goal. We recommend that we start with a simple budget and add complexity with time;

- Planning and allocating resources – This is where we start to get into the detail of our budget. We should work out how much money we have and what we are going to do with it. This will involve gathering data and making decisions on how we will distribute our funds;
- Control and monitoring – Once we have created and implemented our budget, we have to make sure that we stick to it over time, as there is no point of creating one, if we are going to ignore it.

Having a personal budget will help us plan and track our spending. This is an easy step but it will take one month. On the contrary, if we do not have a written budget, most probably we are not aware where our money is going. That is why we need to collect data for a month. This means that over the course of one month we have to write down in detail every single spending we make each day.

When the month is over we will be able to determine the amount of our regular expenses such as bills, food, clothes, gas, rent, credit installment, etc.

What's more, we will also be able to calculate how much money we spend on useless stuff.

Now is the time we make our first budget plan. It must be written down on paper with the purpose that our money has an assignment before the next month begins.

We can do it on the first day of the coming month or at the end of the previous one. After doing the budget for several months, we will be able to forecast our spending for the entire year.

Of course, this is just the beginning. The next thing we will need to do is to track our expenses and make sure that we spend no more than what we have written down in our budget.

> ***"Manage your spending by creating and sticking to a budget."***
>
> ***Alexa Von Tobel***

We must commit ourselves to not adjusting our budget in the middle of the month. Planning at the beginning and following the plan throughout the month is a must.

If this seems difficult and we cannot manage the expenses for the month and at the end there is no money left, it would be a good idea to try and divide our money in four equal amounts and do a weekly instead of a monthly budget.

Having discussed the spending, it is now time to mention the income, i.e. the money we make each month.

> *"A large income is the best recipe for happiness I ever heard of."*
>
> *Jane Austen*

Here we assume that the main source of income for us is our salary. Depending on our contract, it could be paid out once, twice or more times a month. Therefore, we can match the budget-planning period with the interval between two consecutive payments from our employer. Logically, if we spend as much as we make, our budget is balanced. If we spend more – we form a deficit, and if we make more (which certainly is the best option), we accumulate savings.

> *"The deficit is the symptom, but spending is the disease."*
>
> *Jeb Hensarling*

Either way, making a budget has the very positive effect of removing stress, because for the first time we are aware what exactly is happening with our money. We are now in control of our own well-being. Not knowing where our money is going creates stress and uncertainty on subconscious level.

1.1 The traditional way to start

The traditional way to do it is as follows:
Take a piece of paper and write down our income. Check our last six months' paychecks and all other money that we earn. Write down the average amount that we earn per month.
Next, write down the expenses we have. Make sure we list all of them. Most probably they will go under one of the following categories:
- Food;
- Utilities;
- Clothing;
- Transportation;
- Personal;
- Housing;
- Savings;
- Charity;
- Others.

No matter how we categorize our spending, make sure we use the data we have already collected above.

So far so good, but one-month preparation for something that is easy to accomplish is not good enough for everyone. Is there an alternative? The answer is yes!

If we are too impatient to allow 30 days for the process, why not start today? First, divide our salary by 30 – that way we will get an idea of what is the average amount of money we could spend each day. Then don't forget to write down each expense we make during the day. That shouldn't be hard to do.

Now, if we have to make a major payment this very day (rent, credit installment, fill the tank with gas), make sure that we divide it by the number of days we will benefit from it. For example, if this is the rent of our apartment, divide it by 30 and here we go – this is our daily rent. If we pay our credit, again – divide it by 30 and we will have the daily amount of money for covering our debt to the bank. Let's say that we drive two weeks with a full tank of gas – divide the amount we pay for it by 15 and here is our daily gas expense. Again, at the end of the day we need to have spent not more than our daily income.

1.2 Alternative budget tools

Of course, there are a lot of alternative tools that we can use instead of pencil and paper. Here are some ideas:
- Spreadsheet – the idea here is to make the budgeting process easier by using formulas to perform different calculations;
- Software and applications – there are a lot of software solutions and applications written specifically for money management. Products are designed to keep track of individual account information. These software can categorize past expenses and display monthly reports that are useful for budgeting future months;
- Websites – there are several websites created with the sole purpose to help manage personal finances.

It is important to find the best one that will work for us and will allow us to easily track our monthly spending. Having this in mind, we can finally proceed with creating our first budget.

2. Making our first budget

When creating our first budget, it is good to go into detail as much as possible. This will show us exactly where we are with our spending and income. Once we have created a detailed budget, we can analyze it carefully and eventually move to a simpler one. However, seeing the general picture at this initial moment is of key importance to us. We recommend that we do it in three steps: List all our incomes, list all our spending and calculate the balance between them.

When listing our incomes, there are three major categories that we need to consider:
- Employment;
- Investment;
- Miscellaneous.

Employment.

This is the so called direct income – the money we regularly receive in return for our work. Also, this is the most time-consuming way of building up wealth. If we have a Monday-to-Friday job, "Employment" normally is the biggest item in the income (or positive) side of our budget. Below we have listed a number of such income sources:

- Salary paychecks;
- Self-employment income;
- Bonuses;
- Commissions;
- Tax refunds;
- Pension;
- Unemployment;
- Other sources of employment income.

As shown here, apart from our full-time job, we can raise money via part-time jobs, self-employment, commissions, tax refunds (if we qualify for them), etc. Last but not least, having been employed for a certain period of time makes us eligible to receive a guaranteed monthly payment after that – unemployment benefits, pension and so on. Please note that such payments are also forms of compensation for our work.

Investment.

In contrast to "Employment", this item can be described as indirect income (not related to our current job or occupation).

It occurs only if a certain amount of money had been saved (or inherited) in a previous moment and then invested with the purpose to make more money on top of it in the present and in the future.

In other words, to be able to invest, we must start saving first. Here are some examples of investment income:
- Rentals;
- Dividends;
- Interests;
- Other investment income.

Miscellaneous

These types of income don't fall into any of the items discussed above. Below we can see some of the potential sources of miscellaneous income:
- Child support;
- Disability income;
- Alimony;
- Other income;

It is worth mentioning here that "Others" may include random incomes, such as presents, gift cards, etc. They could be received at any moment and therefore are hard to plan in advance.

When we finish filling in the incomes, we will have the total amount of monthly income:

Employment	Comment	Amount	Date
Paycheck 1	John's Salary	1000	1st of month
Paycheck 2	Maria's Salary	2000	1st of month

Total income	3000

Listing our spending – it is recommended to start with the "Four walls" of our spending – food, utilities, clothing and transportation, before moving to the other categories. Here is a list with the main expense categories:
- Food;
- Utilities;
- Clothing;
- Transportation;
- Personal;
- Housing.

Food

The first step when doing our budget expenses is the food. As explained in the Maslow pyramid of motivation, the first thing we need to take care of is the physiological needs – eat, drink, breathe, etc. This is the reason why it is recommended to start with the food section. Here we must calculate what is the amount of money we spend on monthly basis for:
- Groceries;
- Eating out, restaurants;
- Others.

We want to make sure that we have at least the minimum to cover our needs so that our body is functioning normally. It is important not to cut below the minimum in this category as this might affect our health.

Utilities

Once we decide what is the amount we will spend on food we can move to the next category which is utilities. Depending on our situation we might reduce the expenses in this category. We need to put together all the bills and costs for:

- Electricity;
- Water;
- Cable;
- Internet;
- Phone;
- Others.

If we are in debt we can cut several of the expenses from here as some of these can be classified under "wants", not so much in "needs". What we mean is that if we are broke or we have a lot of debt generated we can reduce for example the cable bill. In cases of a lot of debt, we must reduce our expenses to the bare minimum, as every dollar counts in this situation.

Clothing

Once we are done with the utilities we can move to the clothing. Here we can list the following clothing categories:
- Children clothing;
- Adults clothing;
- Cleaning/Laundry;
- Others.

Again here depending on our situation we might want to reduce the extra spending. What we need to try to do here is to stop buying clothes on sale if we really do not need them. We all love the so called "shopping therapy" where we try to buy something new in order to feel happy at least for a while. If we are truly honest to ourselves at least half of our clothes can be categorized in "wants" and the other half will be in "needs". If we are trying to lower our spending this is a great place to get some extra dollars towards our final goal.

Transportation

We all know that having a car is as expensive as having one additional family member. When we are creating a budget we must consider do we really need our current car and the expenses that comes with it:

- Gas;
- Repairs;
- Insurance;
- Car payment;
- Other.

If we are having a loan that we are returning for our vehicle we must consider if we can afford it. In some cases it is better to return our new car and buy a second hand one, that we can pay cash. The purpose of the car is to take us from one place to another. If we are struggling with our money we must really think what are the other options – can we use a public transport, can we reduce the time we spend behind the wheel with walking or riding a bike which are much healthier options.

Personal

Part of every budget should be our personal category. Here we must put everything that we are currently spending money for that is other than our "needs". In this section we usually put our expenses for:
- Education;
- Child care;
- Subscriptions;
- Books;
- Gifts;

- Pocket money;
- Other expenses.

We rarely take account of this category. We spend our money here without thinking and after that we ask ourselves where all our money went. It is easy – the small things make the difference. Once we know what amount of money we are spending per month we can look what we can reduce and what we can postpone for the future when we can afford it.

Housing

The last part of our "needs" that we want to cover is the housing category. Housing is fundamental part of the Maslow's pyramid and it is under the security stage. In order for us to feel safe it is recommend to live in our own house even if we are paying mortgage. The expenses we associate with housing include:
- Rent;
- Mortgage;
- Taxes;
- Repairs;
- Others;

We cannot reduce a lot of expenses here, but we can think how we can get debt free faster with paying our housing debts faster.

That pretty much sums it up as far as our regular monthly expenses are concerned. However, in order for us to go down the path to becoming rich, we need to perceive the following two items as part of our expenses:
- Savings;
- Charity.

Savings

When we have built our budget in order to lower the stress caused by money, it is recommended to have some savings for rainy days. Emergency fund is something that we need to think about as it will reduce our stress significantly. It is recommended to have an emergency fund equal to our spending for 5-6 months period. This will guarantee that if we have a health issue or we lose our job we will feel secure and we will go through the difficult times much easier.

Charity

Last thing we want to put in our budget is the charities we are doing at the moment. Giving money to other people to help them is one of the end goals for many people. It is very good to help the others but we must make sure that we have enough to take care for ourselves before we help others. For many people putting the needs of others is much more important than having financial stability for themselves. Although this is great act of human kindness it is not the best solution. We know that one of the basic instructions when we are flying with a plane is that in case of emergency we put our oxygen mask before we put the one to the kids around us. We cannot help anyone if we do not take care for ourselves first.

Theoretically speaking, both Savings and Charity require a surplus (more income than costs) in our budget. But if we do it the other way around and think of the money we save and/or donate as just another expense, we are in a better position to gradually build wealth.

For example, we know that every month we have to spend around $100 for our electricity bill. Not paying it is out of question – if we don't, the provider will shut it down. Now think about saving $100 monthly – are we going to wait and see if we will have the extra money at the end of the month, or will we put it away the minute we receive it (just like the $100 for electricity)? Undoubtedly, we are more likely to form a good savings fund, if we choose the second option. All this is more psychology than economics but, after all, we try to change our mindset more than anything else.

Expenses summary

Category	Budgeted	Actual spent
Food		
Utilities		
Clothing		
Transportation		
Personal		
Housing		
Savings		
Charity		

Total expenses		

Once we have all the detailed information for our expenses we can summarize them for better tracking. If we decide to use budget system such as the envelope one, these categories can be our main ones.

The last step is to calculate the totals and to get the final balance:

Totals	
Total income	
Total expenses	
Balance	

The last step here will be to summarize the entire budget and to calculate the totals. Later we will look at the different scenarios we can have for a negative, zero or positive budget balance.

3. Budget planning and strategies

"The budget is not just a collection of numbers, but an expression of our values and aspirations."

Jacob Lew

There are many ways to make our first budget plan, but nevertheless try to keep it simple. With time we can improve it and make it more complicated. We will look at the first steps that we deem important in drafting our budget. There are many strategies out there and that is because people are different and if something works for someone, that doesn't mean it will work for everyone. Below we will try to cover the most often used budgeting strategies, so that we can determine what is the best one for us and our situation. The most popular ones are:
- Zero-based;
- Envelope system;

- 60% solution;
- 50/30/20;
- 80/20;
- Automated budget.

3.1 Zero-based budget

The idea behind zero-based budget a.k.a. zero-sum budget is to put us in control of our income and expenses. To achieve financial sustainability is different story though. In this regard, heading to a zero-based budget should definitely be our mid- to long term objective. The ultimate goal of the zero-based budget is to strike a balance between what we earn and what we spend. Which means that our expenses should always be equal to our income. The steps to do a zero-based budget are as follows:

- Write down our monthly income;
- Write down our monthly expenses;
- Write down any seasonal/irregular expenses – here we should include things that happen once or twice a year – birthdays, Christmas, family vacation, etc. After we plan this, we can divide the total to 12 and add the result in our budget. This way every month we will

add 1/12 of the yearly-based irregular expenses;
- Subtract our monthly income and expenses.

There are three case scenarios for our budget:
- Income and expenses are equal;
- Income is higher than the expenses;
- Expenses are higher than the income.

In the first scenario, all our monthly expenses (incl. the payments which cover our debt each month) are equal to our monthly income.

The second scenario is the best one as we have a surplus, meaning that after we have paid out all our expenses, including all of our debt, we would end up with a certain amount of extra money. Since it is important for this method to give every dollar a name, we need to put the surplus in action. We can add it to our savings, cover debt, etc.

The third scenario is the worst one, but still happening more often than not. Once we create our budget plan we have more expenses than income. In this case we have several options to clear our debts:
- Finding additional job or/and work extra hours;
- Reduce the monthly expenses;
- Combination of the two options above.

We have created 2 sample budgets to visualize those options:

Before	
Income	
Paycheck 1	1000
Paycheck 2	2000

Expenses	
Food	500
Utilities	700
Clothing	200
Transportation	300
Personal	200
Housing	500
Savings	0
Charity	0
Debt 1 - CC	200
Debt 2 - CC	300
Debt 3 - Car	300
Debt 4 - Bank	200
Debt 5 - Student	100

Balance	
Income	3000
Expences	3500
Balance	-500

After	
Income	
Paycheck 1	1000
Paycheck 2	2000
Paycheck 3	300

Expenses	
Food	400
Utilities	500
Clothing	100
Transportation	100
Personal	100
Housing	500
Savings	0
Charity	0
Debt 1 - CC	200
Debt 2 - CC	300
Debt 3 - Car	300
Debt 4 - Bank	200
Debt 5 - Student	100

Balance	
Income	3300
Expences	2800
Balance	500

On the left hand side, the budget has formed a deficit of $500 at the end of the month. On the right hand side, we see that person X has managed to combine a new source of income of $300 with the reduction of some expenses of $700. These extra $1000 transform the deficit of $500 into a surplus of $500.

This budget strategy is great for people who have debt and aim to get rid of it as fast as possible. It is suitable for persons that hate to waste money and prefer to feel as much in control as possible. Of course, it is also recommended for people who want to have a lot of money for fun and entertainment.

3.2 Envelope system

The envelope system a.k.a. Clip system or Cash-only budget is one of the oldest and well known budget strategies. The main idea here is that we use cash for different categories of our budget, and we keep that cash tucked away in envelopes. The monitoring and tracking of our spending with this system is easy as we have visibility on them at all times. It's a good idea to use the envelope system for items that tend to bust our budget such as groceries, entertainment, clothing, etc. For all these categories we will need to create an envelope and allocate the amount of money we planned in the beginning of the month.

The most important thing here is that we pay for these categories only in cash. If there is nothing in our envelope we just don't spend till next month. Of course, as every other budget system in the first three months we can make certain adjustments until we get the right amounts to allocate for each envelope. Once we have a stable budget, if our grocery envelope is empty, it is not allowed for us to take money from other envelopes. As already stated, we cannot pay with credit cards for any of these categories. If we need to buy food, make sure that we take the relevant amount of money from the envelope before we go shopping. If we don't have cash in us, we just do not buy anything – simple as that.

As we can see, this strategy is not as strict as the zero-based budget and it is mostly focused on the variable expenses that change every month.

Here are the basic steps related to this method:
- Stop using credit cards and pay only cash;
- Create a budget – this system does not include a methodology how to create our budget, so it is recommend that we create a budget the traditional way;
- Separate our fixed from our variable expenses. For the fixed expenses, such as rent, mortgage, etc. we do not need to create envelopes at all;
- Divide the variable expenses into different categories, such as – food, clothing, entertainment, etc;

- Create an envelope for each of these categories and fill it with the amount of money that we planned in our budget at the beginning of the month (or when we receive our paycheck);
- During the month, pay in cash by taking money only from the relevant envelope;
- Revise our spendings before the next month. In case there is money left in one or more of the envelopes, we can use the surplus to cover some debt or we can add it to our savings. We can also reward ourselves for making the month under our budget, this will help us with the inner motivation and will keep us going with this strategy;
- Refill the envelopes with the next payment and start all over again.

This strategy is for people that tend to overspend and easily lose track of their variable expenses.

3.3 60% Solution Budget

The "60% solution" budget was created by Richard Jenkins. He invented this strategy after realizing that the traditional way of making and tracking budget was not ideal for him.

The main idea of this strategy is to prevent overspending, as it leads to debt. In other words, we structure our budget in a way that we do not have to take account of every penny spent.

This strategy is based on the concept that the things that most affect our spending are the large, irregular expenses – like vacations, major repairs and holidays, and that we rarely overspend on small things, such as dining out, entertainment, clothes, etc. If we find this way of thinking reasonable, then this strategy will work great for us.

The logic of "60% Solution" is the following:

- 60% of all our income should go to the so called "Committed expenses" category. This percentage may vary though – for example, it can be 50% or 70% depending on the household. These expenses include:
  - Basic food and clothing needs;
  - Essential household expenses;
  - Insurance premiums;
  - All of our bills;
  - All of our taxes.

The rest of our money is divided into four equal categories. If our committed expenses are 60%, then the allocation for each of those categories will be 10%. It is important to make sure that

these amounts are deducted automatically from our paycheck or right after receiving our monthly payment:
- Retirement savings;
- Mid-term to long-term savings;
- Short-term savings;
- Fun money.

Retirement savings

This is self-explanatory. Note that 10% is the minimum recommended amount to be invested in our retirement. A common mistake of young people is to underestimate the importance of this category. They often think of retirement as some event from the distant future, that has almost nothing to do with them. Then, as the years go by, everyone gets more and more concerned with it, but on many occasions it proves to be too late to guarantee a decent retirement plan for themselves.

Mid-term to long-term savings

For example, this money could be saved for buying a new car. It should not be easily accessible, so that we are not constantly tempted to spend it. One way to do that is to open a 1-, 2- or 5-year deposit in a bank. If we withdraw the money before the maturity date (i.e. the end of the period) of our deposit, we would lose the accumulated interest. That will make us think twice whether it is worth it to simply spend the money on the first thing we see, or it is better not only to keep it intact but also to earn a little extra (or at least protect it from inflation). Certainly, we can use the money in the case of an emergency.

Short-term savings

These are meant to cover the irregular expenses – such as vacations, holidays, etc. The money should be within our grasp, because we will use it much more often, compared to the previous two categories.

Fun money

We can spend it on anything we like during the month, as long as the total doesn't exceed 10% of our income.
This strategy is for everyone who believes that large expenses are the ones that do most of the damage. It is good for people that do not make impulsive decisions and spending, and it is not applicable for the ones that spend without thinking.

3.4 50/30/20 Budget

The 50/30/20 rule for spending and saving was introduced by Elizabeth Warren and her daughter Amelia Warren Tyagi in the book "All Your Worth: The Ultimate Lifetime Money Plan.". This is a great budget strategy for everyone who thinks that traditional budgeting is boring and for people that want to have more freedom in spending. It is a fairly simple way to do our budget. It is based on the "rule of thumb". The specifics of this approach is that the income we can use is calculated after taxes (this is our so called net income) and is to be spent on the following:
- 50% – necessities/needs;
- 30% – wants;
- 20% – financial goals.

50% – necessities/needs

The necessities again are the "four walls" of our financial house – food, utilities, clothing and transportation. They should be 50% of our planned budget. Needs are those bills that we absolutely must pay and are necessary for survival. These include rent or <u>mortgage</u> payments, car payments, groceries, insurance, health care, minimum debt payment and utilities.

30% – wants

Wants are all the things we spend money on, that are not essential. Basically, wants are all those little extras that make life more enjoyable and entertaining. It is important to be able to determine what spending qualify as needs and what as wants. Remember that getting what we want might sometimes be opposite to getting what we need.

20% – financial goals

The last 20% of our income after taxes should be allocated for our financial goals – savings and investments. This includes adding money to an emergency fund in a bank savings account, investing in the stock market, etc.

This is a very good strategy to start with, for people without debt who want to keep their budget as simple as possible. Have in mind that this should not be used if we have a lot of debts.

3.5 80/20 Budget

What to do, if we are not able to differentiate the wants from the necessities as required in the "50/30/20" rule?

The answer is simple – a "80/20" budget. This is the simplest budget that we can make. In analogy to the 50/30/20, it is important at the beginning of each month to deduct 20% of our income for savings and investments. This is the easiest strategy, giving us the most freedom in comparison to the others.

This strategy is only for people that are debt free and live in their own house. If this is not our case, we recommend that we use another method for budgeting.

3.6 Automated budget

Last but not least, we want to mention the automated budget a.k.a. the no-budget budget. This can be used separately or in a combination with any of the above.

The idea here is to automate as much of our spendings as possible. This means to set automated payments going directly from our paycheck for things like mortgage, rent, bills, savings and retirement, etc. By using this method, after all the automated expenses are covered, whatever is left in our bank account we can spend any way we want. It is easier to track what is left.

This budget is not for everyone and we recommend to be combined with another budgeting strategy.

In conclusion, depending on our current situation, we can evaluate what is the best budget for us. Use the "Zero-based", if we want full control of our money, we do not want to spend on unnecessary things or if we are in a lot of debt. Use the "Envelope system", if our biggest issue with spending are the little expenses through the month. Use the "60% solution", if we do not have issues with the little things, but we struggle when it comes to the big expenses. The last three methods are for people that do not want to make a complicated budget and are debt free.

4. Monitoring and controlling our budget

"Budgeting has only one rule: Do not go over budget."

Leslie Tayne

After we finish with the planning and allocating resources and our first budget is ready we need to start monitoring and controlling it.

Our budget is a plan and things don't always go as we want them to. We need to start monitoring our activities on a regular basis (days, weeks, months) to see where we are in relation to our targets.

In order to do this we are going to introduce the term "variances". This is the difference between the planned and the actual results. This differences can be positive or negative. Negative variance means that we spent more than we have planned and positive variance means that we spent less. For example if we spent $100 more on our car, this is negative variance. If we went on a holiday and planned to spend $3000, but we spend only $2800, this means that we underspent and there is $200 positive variance.

Overspending is not something we want to do for obvious reasons: we cannot spend more money than we have in our budget. If we overspend on one item, we may need to cut back on other areas and this may impact on achieving our objectives.

Positive variances are just as important as overspends. If we have come in under budget, we may be leaving out something that was important and not using our money in the best way possible.

Reviewing our budget on regular basis enables us to track the overall effect that certain changes in our plans have had on our financial performance. It also tells us where we are wandering off track. Reviewing variances is also an early warning mechanism so that there are no huge surprises at the end of the budget period. Variances not only tell us if there is a problem but also the size of the problem. Keep in mind that not all variances will be preventable.

By tracking and monitoring our budget we can stay in control and demonstrate good management of our activities and their financial impacts.

Here are some tips how to monitor our budget:
- Monitor our budget on a regular basis. If things are going off course, we need to know about it as soon as possible so that we take any necessary action. Mark budget monitoring as a top priority item. Set a specific date and time in our calendar every week to review and track it;
- Do not leave corrective action until it is too late to do anything;

- Think through any planned corrective action. Might it have any undesirable side effects? Will it happen in time for the next monitor report or is it likely that we will not see the results for more than two periods?
- If we believe that we are heading for an overspend, then take actions. The more time we have to do something about it, the more likely we are to recover the situation.

DEBT FREE

"What can be added to the happiness of a man who is in health, out of debt, and has a clear conscience?"

Adam Smith

Once our budget is ready the next step should be, although this is not mandatory for the high risk strategies, getting out of debt.
Removing the burden of debt from our shoulders will clear the mind and will make our decisions less dependent on internal emotions.

1. Debt or investment

> *"All financial institutions live and die by their liquidity. We are a financial institution. The fact that many people don't think about it is beyond me. It is the essence of what we do."*
>
> *Ken Griffin*

There has always been an argument if we should pay our debt first and then invest or to invest while paying the minimum payments for our debts. When we talk about debt, we certainly see it as money borrowed and used some time ago to cover expenses that the borrower could not afford. Investment, in contrast, is money that one has got and has decided not to spend on goods and services, but to try and multiply by doing or supporting some business activity.

It is worth mentioning that, according to a well-known economic definition, in order for the system to be in equilibrium, the total amount of investments should be equal to the total amount of savings in the country for the same period of time. Simply said, for money to be invested, it must be saved first. Here comes the tricky part – the one who has saved a certain amount of money may or may not be the one to invest it. When we think about it, we will realize that we can take a loan (from a financial institution or from another person) only because they already have the money available (or in other words – saved).

Coming back to the "debt or investment" dilemma – can we be in debt and make investments at the same time? The answer is yes. However, we have to be very strict about whose money it is and what it is used for. For example, if we earn some extra money and decide to invest it instead of paying back our debt, we will continue to "pay the price" for using somebody else's money.

Now is the right time to explain another economic term – the so called *"opportunity cost"*. When we make a decision to do something, there is always another option (or even a number of options) which we consider a "second choice" or an alternative to what we choose to do. Every one of us comes across such choices on a daily basis and makes many of them almost automatically.

However, when we talk about money making, it is very important to weigh our alternatives – the amount of money that could be earned by our second choice is the opportunity cost of our first choice.

So what is the opportunity cost of making an investment when we are still in debt? It is the money for interest that we could have saved by paying back the debt. Certainly, if the investment brings back more than the potentially saved interest, it is worth it.

Of course, different people prefer to use different strategies. When choosing the best solution for ourselves we recommend that we take into consideration the financial, as well as the emotional aspects of the problem. Have in mind that:

- Debt carries stress and risk with itself;
- We might be able to get a better deal in the market.

We should always make our decisions with a clear understanding that financial problems are the main source of stress and family issues. We have to consider this and try to find the best formula for us. The improvement of our financial status must not be realized at the cost of poor health or spoiled relationship with the loved ones.

If being in debt stresses us out and we are losing our sleep over it, don't be afraid to prioritize paying it off, even if the numbers argue for investing. If stress is not an issue for us, the lower the interest rate on our debt, the more we should focus on investing (because of its lower *opportunity cost* in this scenario). Anyway, if we would like to do both simultaneously, we can split the extra money in half between investment and debt.

Of course, if we are debt-free, we can skip this chapter entirely, although we are advised to approach our indebtedness as a dynamic rather than a static category. That's simply because in many unexpected situations we may have to take or pay back a loan (not necessarily ours, for instance) in a matter of hours, even minutes.

2. Basic debt free strategies

"Pay off your debt first. Freedom from debt is worth more than any amount you can earn."

Mark Cuban

There are different ways to attack our debt, each of them having its advantages and disadvantages. Below we have listed some of the most popular methods to become debt free:
- Smallest to highest monthly payment;
- Highest to smallest monthly payment;

- Highest to smallest interest rate;
- Highest to smallest emotional engagement;
- Smallest to highest balance.

Smallest to highest monthly payment

The first strategy is based on a balanced budget with a dedicated section for covering debt money.

Once we have the extra money, we start paying the smallest debts first.

After we've paid something off, move on to the next debt on the list. Add the extra amount (economized after clearing the smallest payment) to the second smallest payment and pay it faster. Then move on to the third until we have them all paid out.

In order to illustrate this strategy we will use the data from the budget above. We have a total of five debts:

Debt	Minimum payment	Months left	Total payment
Debt 1 - CC	200	20	4000
Debt 2 - CC	300	36	10800
Debt 3 - Car	300	20	6000
Debt 4 - Bank	200	60	12000
Debt 5 - Student Loan	100	120	12000

First thing we need to do is to arrange them by the smallest minimum payment per month. In case there are debts with the same minimum payment, we will arrange by the next column – Months left.

From the budget exercise we were able to create surplus of $500. Using this strategy, the surplus amount is added to the smallest payment, in order to get rid of the debt as fast as possible.

In the example below we can see that now the actual payment amount for debt 5 is now $600 instead of $100. This means that we will return the Student loan for 20 months instead of 120 months.

For all the other debts we will keep paying the minimum amount.

With the payment of month 20 we can see that we have managed to return Debt 5, 1 and 3.

Debt	Minimum payment	Months left	Total payment	Actual payment	Completion month
Debt 5 - Student Loan	100	120	12000	100+500	20
Debt 1 - CC	200	20	4000	200	20
Debt 4 - Bank	200	60	12000	200	
Debt 3 - Car	300	20	6000	300	20
Debt 2 - CC	300	36	10800	300	

On month 21 we have already returned Debt 5, 1 and 3. The total surplus now is $1100. This amount is added to Debt 4, so its actual payment becomes $1300. This debt will be gone after the 27th monthly payment. On the 27th month the last payment to cover Debt 4 will be only 200. Finally, we use all the extra money to cover Debt 2:

Debt	Minimum payment	Months left	Total payment	Actual payment	Completion month
Debt 5 - Student Loan	100	0	0		20
Debt 1 - CC	200	0	0		20
Debt 4 - Bank	200	40	8000	1300	27
Debt 3 - Car	300	0	0		20
Debt 2 - CC	300	16	4800	300	

Thus, with the 28th monthly payment all the debts will be covered:

Debt	Minimum payment	Months left	Total payment	Actual payment	Completion month
Debt 5 - Student Loan	100	0	0		20
Debt 1 - CC	200	0	0		20
Debt 4 - Bank	200	40	8000		27
Debt 3 - Car	300	0	0		20
Debt 2 - CC	300	9	1600	1600	28

To sum up the results achieved, with this strategy we have paid back the same amount of money for all 4 debts, but we became debt free on the 28th month instead of 120th, i.e. 92 months in advance. In other words, we have managed to save approximately 77% of the time required to pay back all the debts – a remarkable success.

Furthermore, if we clear debts 2,4 and 5 earlier, depending on the debt contract terms and conditions, we can pay less money for interest.

This strategy is logical, easy to follow and will take some pressure off our wallet with every debt paid.

Its biggest benefit being that we enjoy the results in the soonest time possible – when we are still highly motivated. Once we see that the smallest debt is gone, a new impulse of motivation will come and will keep us going.

Of course, the strategy suggests that we do all that with the extra money we make or with the money saved by optimizing our budget. Otherwise it would simply not work.

In conclusion, using Strategy 1, we get debt free significantly sooner than initially planned, also saving money from the smaller amount of overall interest due.

Highest to smallest monthly payment

The second strategy is the opposite to the first one. The idea behind it is that the results would come later, but then a huge amount of money would be released for the smaller debt. Once the highest debt is removed, all the smaller ones will be covered pretty fast.

This strategy is based upon the psychological fact that we are most motivated at the beginning of a new task and that is when we can achieve best results. Along these lines, the more we pay out in total, the lower our credit exposition will be.

So, as time goes on, even if we find it hard to continue with the second strategy and move to the first one, the general picture of our indebtedness will be better and we will certainly benefit from it.

Highest to smallest interest rate

The strategy based on the interest rate a.k.a. "Debt avalanche" is one of the most popular strategies in the financial world. This strategy is one of the best, if not the best, mathematically efficient debt free strategies. The reasoning behind the third strategy is that covering the debt with highest interest rate will reduce the total amount of money we have to pay in the long run. It has its grounding in one of the fundamental principles of the financial management called interest rate optimization.

In this strategy we start by paying off the debt with the highest interest rate and go down through the rest until we reach the lowest interest rate debt. Let's illustrate it with the following example:

We have three monthly installments to pay. Each of them is $100, but the interest rate is 4, 8 and 15% respectively. Now our average interest rate is 4 + 8 + 15 / 3 = 9%. Meaning that the banks take $9 on every $100 in credit. Say we follow the third strategy and manage to cover the credit with 15% interest rate. Then the average percentage would be 4 + 8 / 2 = 6%. The positive effect on our personal finances is that on every $100 in credit, from now on we will have to pay $6 rather than $9.

There is an additional advantage in tackling the debt with highest interest rate. Every credit product we take from a bank comes together with a payment plan. Normally, the monthly instalments are equal. If we examine the plan closely, we will find out that each instalment comprises of two elements – principal and interest. Although exceptions exist, the relative weight of the interest as part of the instalment is the highest in the first payment period and almost non-existent in the last one. Analogically, the principal we cover with our first payment is way smaller than the one we clear with the last one.

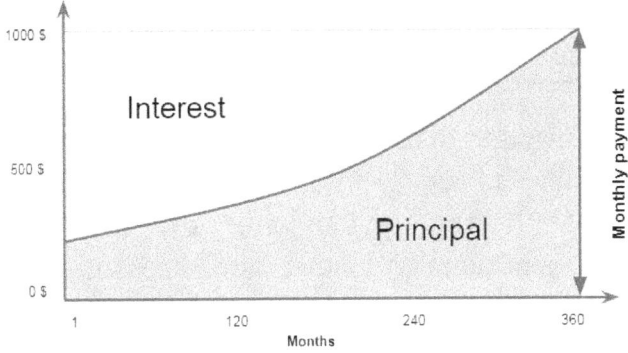

If we compare the payment plans of our 3 credit products, we will easily discover that the "Interest" zone of the graph shown above is much bigger for the credit with 15% interest rate than for the ones with 4% and 8%. It means that we are to pay a lot more to clear it, than the amount of money actually taken from the bank.

The benefits of this strategy are that we get out of debt in the most efficient way – since we attack the highest interest rate first, we will pay less money in total for interest.

The downside of this method is that it is mathematically based and does not take into account the emotional side of the debt repayment process.

Highest to smallest emotional engagement

The highest to lowest emotional engagement strategy a.k.a. "Debt tsunami" is a theory opposite to the previous one, as we attack the most emotionally loaded and stressful debt, regardless of its mathematical logic. The idea here is to start with the most emotionally impactful and gradually move to the least impactful debt.

The name "Debt tsunami" is based on the notion that tsunamis like our emotions are very hard to detect.

Always bear in mind that for most people, the process of debt reduction is really emotional. Knowing that, we have two choices to attack our debt. Either remove all the emotions from the process completely – this is what the previous strategy (highest interest first) is based on, or evaluate our emotions, identify with them, and leverage them to help us – which is what this strategy is all about. So here is how this method works:

- Evaluate how we feel for each and every debt separately. Try to answer the following questions as honest as possible:

- How do we feel about the creditor? Is he / she part of the family?
- How strong is our connection?
- How long will it take to pay it off?
- How much stress is this debt generating to us?
- How much of a burden is this particular debt to our financial life?
• Reorder our list, based on the debts' potential emotional impact – Order the debts by how it will feel to eliminate them;
• Start handling debts from the highest emotional impact to the lowest one.

The main advantage of the method is that we get rid of the most stressful debt first. We all know that personal finance is more than just mathematics. But, of course, this might not be the best option from economic point of view.

Lowest to highest balance

The lowest to highest balance strategy a.k.a. "The debt snowball" is a strategy popularized by Dave Ramsey. The strategy is not the best from mathematical point of view like the "highest interest first" but it takes into account emotions and motivation. It is among the most efficient ones when we talk about earlier repayment of our debts.

The idea of the strategy is to pay the lowest balance first, regardless of its interest rate and emotional ranking. The concept here is based on the premises that the faster we see the first results, the more motivated we will be on subconscious and psychological level to carry on and clear our debts.

With this strategy we start by attacking the one with the smallest balance, in which we put all the extra money we have. For the rest of our debts we pay just the minimum monthly payment. Once we pay the smallest one, we move to the next in the list. To this next debt we add the minimum payment of the one that we have already paid, along with the additional extra money we have been able to generate through optimizing our budget.

3. Supplementary debt free strategies

> *"Debt is one person's liability, but another person's asset."*
>
> ***Paul Krugman***

Along with the basic strategies we have already described, there are several supplementary ones that we can do along with them. These supplementary strategies are good to be used together with any of the strategies previously described, except for the zero-based budget. That is because when we implement that budget plan, we put name to every dollar and it would be very hard to squeeze off any additional money (which is needed for the supplementary strategies). Another thing worth mentioning is that some people prefer them to the basic ones. This is by no means a great idea, as the supplementary strategies are not invented to replace a budget.

In the following pages we shall briefly describe 3 of them:
- Found money a.k.a. "Debt snowflake";
- Saving our change;
- Penny in a jar challenge.

Found money a.k.a. "Debt snowflake"

This strategy is a good way to improve our debt repayment. It is based on the idea that if we find any amount of money, let's say in our old jacket's pocket instead of buying something impulsively we put it towards paying off our debts. As we can guess this is not a strategy that will generate in the long run, but if done for a longer period can speed up our overall time to get out of debt. Benefit of this method is based on the human psychology by showing us fast progress. It is also good for improving the way we think of how we spend our money and think more critically how we manage our finance.

Saving our change

A lot of people use this strategy to collect money to buy something expensive or reduce debt. The idea is quite simple – we put all the coins that we get as change from the store. The amount is small and we usually do not think a lot for the coins in the pocket. Again if this is done in a longer period of time it can generate quite a lot of money. If we are going to use this as a debt free strategy we need to set a fixed period of time when we are going to take the coins out and add it to our monthly debt payment. This period depends on us and can be monthly, once every three months or even once a year.

Penny in a jar challenge

This is similar to the previous one but it is based on a strict payment system. Every day for a year (365 days), we should put pennies in a jar equivalent to the number of days spent on the challenge. For example: Day 1 = 1 penny, Day 10 = 10 pennies, Day 365 = $3.65. At the end of the year we should have at least $667 in her jar. Since this starts off with such a little amount and it's increased with such a little amount every day at some point it will become a habit.

As we can see, there are many ways for us to create our first budget. To make those strategies more understandable and easier to implement, we have tried to match them with different psychological and emotional profiles that people have. Needless to say, none of this budgeting methods is a panacea – they all have their strong and weak points. However, with the right attitude and motivation, pretty soon we will be able to find the type of budget which suits us best.

Ok, all this makes sense, but what is the key message of this Chapter? – If we are determined to become rich, it is an absolute must to have a personal budget.

Right away, we will start benefiting from the short term effects of our decision. We will stop asking ourselves "Where did all my money go?", as it will no more be randomly spent on overpriced stuff that we don't need. We will notice that we are in a better mood much more often, our self-confidence will grow and we won't be afraid whether we could afford the expenses that are to be made.

In the long run, having a budget will put our finances in order, improve our spending discipline and allow us to gradually build wealth.

Both our incomes and our expenses will change over time – that is perfectly normal. If we manage to keep them within a logical framework which is in line with our main financial goals, there is nothing to worry about.

MAKING OUR MONEY WORK FOR US

"Don't stay in bed, unless you can make money in bed."

George Burns

After learning what money is, putting our personal finances in order through the creation of a budget plan and taking our first steps to a debt free life, we have reached the point to make our money work for us. As soon as this process starts, we will gradually build wealth and feel more and more confident about it with each passing day.

1. Active and passive sources of income

"You become financially free when your passive income exceeds your expenses."

T. Harv Eker

The most important thing in the money making game is to make sure that we have more money coming in, than we have going out. The first step – understanding where our money comes from, is made by defining the difference between active income and passive income.

1.1 Active income

The active income is an income we get from trading our time and performing active efforts to earn money. Examples include:
- Working on a traditional job from 9 to 5;
- Working part time;
- Freelance;
- Own business in which we are actively involved.

Basically, it is everything that we need to do repeatedly and constantly to ensure that the income won't stop coming.

Earning active income typically carries lower risk and therefore is the preferable source of income. When we spoke about motivation, we mentioned that security is one of the basic things that we as individuals try to guarantee for ourselves.

Another benefit of the active income is its better predictability. Again, this is based on the human nature to reduce chaos and uncertainty. If we rely only on active income, we close ourselves in our comfort zone. However, that can prevent us from looking for new opportunities and can limit our earning potential.

1.2 Passive income

The passive income is everything in which we invest time, money or both only once, but from that point on it starts generating money for us by itself.

There are several main sources of passive income:

- Royalty – books, app creation, etc.;
- Returns – shares, stocks, notes, interests, art, gold, property. These are things that we think will increase their value with time;
- Investing in other people's business – Startups and any business that do not require our presence;

- Rent – property, vehicle, equipment;
- Rights – franchise, licensees, brand.

Here is the time to mention several interesting things we came across through the years. Passive income is a great source of income but it comes along with a certain level of insecurity and might be considered dangerous by some. Also at this point we must understand that passive income isn't as passive as it might seem. Like everything else, it has upsides and downsides.

Passive income upsides

Passive income is great because of the following:

- We are not going to lie – it is wonderful to get our first $5-$10 per day by doing nothing;
- We get paid even when we are on a vacation;
- Our passive daily income may become so big, that we would be able to quit our job;
- We are our own boss;
- We have the freedom to make our own working schedule;
- The increase of our income depends on our own effort. We can double and triple

our passive income in a month, something we cannot do if we work for someone else 40 hours a week.

Passive income downsides

So far we mentioned the upsides of the passive income, but it is not perfect. Let's see some of its downsides:

- The passive income is not as passive as we might think. We will need to constantly take care of it to maintain its current status. We cannot leave our passive income on its own for a long time – we should do at least a minimum effort to make sure everything is up and running;
- We will not start earning money (in other words, gaining passive income) right away. Several months, even years can pass before we start receiving a stable small amount on a regular basis;
- We should invest a lot of time today to get results in the future. In most cases, we will have to sacrifice our free time, while working for an active income (working for someone else);
- We will need to work harder and longer. If we do this together with an active

income related job, our working hours per week will increase to 60 or more;
- Once we start living only on passive income, we will give up part of the security that the regular job provides. All in all, this is not a big deal, but on a subconscious level it might generate fear and stress;
- Everything is changing too fast. If something is profitable today, it will attract other people to start doing the same. That would undoubtedly decrease our profit. Therefore, we should constantly look for alternative sources of passive income;
- Passive income can make us lazy – if we live without a schedule and money come in without any effort, our motivation can drop drastically.

2. Creating our active/passive income portfolio

"At any time you're free to use active income, passive income, or hybrid strategies — or any combo of these you wish. You don't have to quit your active income job to set up streams of passive income."

Steve Pavlina

Now, when we know what are the characteristics and the main differences of active and passive income, it is time to decide what portfolio we should create.

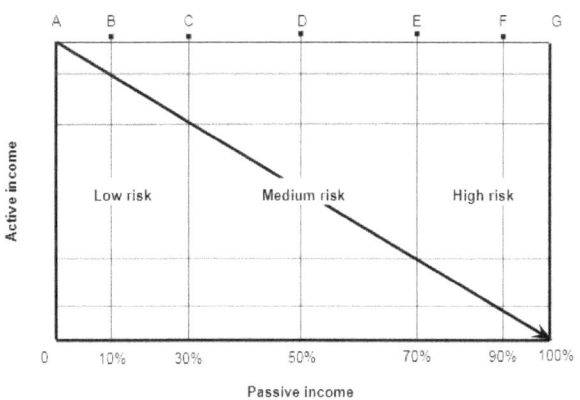

Although most of the people live on only one income source – active (A-B) or passive (F-G), we would recommend that we balance our portfolio to have both active and passive sources of income. The idea is to create a portfolio that fully reflects our financial goals.

Having said that, it is good to know that the portfolio theory is an important part of modern economics. It covers a lot more aspects of our economic activity than income sources.

In short, it helps us minimize risk while optimizing our returns by combining a number of things in a given ratio. Depending on what those things are, we can create:

- An income portfolio – just like the one in the example above;
- An investment portfolio – it is a mix of different investment assets (gold, shares, bonds, foreign currencies, real estate, etc.);
- A debt portfolio – it seeks the right balance between our debt payments, debt periods, interest rates.

We can elaborate on and further extend the list of portfolios, but the main point here is different – to make us understand the logic behind it and put it to work in our everyday choices. To do that, always look for a balanced decision; have more than one option, more than one scenario; make a back-up plan; design an exit strategy, etc.

Have in mind that in life, just as in economics, there are ups and downs. The single moment, the one-off profit or loss, has a much lower impact on our well-being than the long-term trend, the direction in which we are heading.

3. Introduction to Investing – Net Present Value

"Investing money is the process of committing resources in a strategic way to accomplish a specific objective."

Alan Gotthardt

When we decide to invest, we must take into consideration that "$1 today is more than $1 tomorrow." The meaning behind this basic principle of economics has been explained above. So, by making an investment, we put our money to work right now and aim to extract economic profit at a future moment. To calculate today's money equivalent of an investment with a given term (months, years) is to calculate its "Net Present Value". It shows the current value of all negative and positive money flows that arise over time as a result of investing, after being discounted by the so-called discount factor. Properly setting the discount rate is of key importance to the ultimate success of the venture. For example, we can decide that our discount rate will be the expected return from second best option for investing our money (we touched on the subject when discussing the opportunity cost). If the net present value is positive, the investment is economically justified.

Net present value is calculated as follows:

$$NPV = \sum_{t=1}^{T} \frac{C_t}{(1+r)^t} - C_o$$

where:
NPV – net present value;
t – period of time;
C – money flow;
r – rate of return (discount rate).

By investing, the investor originally formed a negative money flow C_o. Until the investment deadline, he/she receives one or more positive money flows $C_1, C_2, ..., C_t$. Each of them is discounted with the discount factor, according to the above formula.

Let the person X invest in a property the sum of $100000. The investment period is 15 years, the expected annual rent to be received is $10000 and the discount rate is 3%. Then:

$$NPV = \frac{10000}{(1+0.03^1)} + \frac{10000}{(1+0.03^2)} + \cdots + \frac{10000}{(1+0.03^{15})} - 100000$$

NPV = 119380 − 100000 = 19380, therefore the profit from the investment is $19380.

As seen from the example, the aggregate rental income of 15 years, amounting to $150000, is reduced to $119380, with regard to the time value of money.

Our example can certainly be expanded and adjusted, so as to meet the objective economic circumstances as much as possible – then the calculations will become even more precise:

- It is possible to add more to the initial investment cost over the years. Then for each of them we have to subtract from the expected $10000 inflow the amount of the additional investment and discount the result obtained. For instance, during the 7th year we make some property improvements at the amount of $6000. Then the net money flow for that year will amount to $4000, which after discounting is equivalent to $3252 today. The final financial effect for the investor will be a profit of $14501

instead of $19380. Have in mind that the actual rent income may also vary for each of the years and that would change the end result as well;
- The rate of discount might be different for one or more of the 15 periods, due to:
  - changes in the economic environment;
  - inflationary and deflationary influence;
  - an additional risk premium the investor wants to calculate, and so on.
- The Net Present Value model can be successfully applied for longer and shorter than 1 year periods – the above example can also be calculated on a monthly basis (under this hypothesis, the periods will be 180 rather than 15). However, it is important to set a discount rate that is comparable to the new shorter period. For example, our 3% annual discount rate should be divided by 12 and for each of the months it is 3/12 = 0.25%;
- It is possible to adjust the flows according to the resulting tax effects – savings and/or liabilities related to the taxes applicable to the investment.

It should be made clear that net present value is only one of the many tools to assess the profitability of the investment. Using its formula, we are also able to answer the following questions:

What return on investment should be sought, in order to make a profit?

What is the right time frame for the investment to be profitable?

Thus, with a high degree of reliability, different investment alternatives can be compared and the results – calculated within a preselected time horizon.

A good approach when making an investment is to do it in harmony with the rest of our financial activities – budget planning, spending and saving money, paying out debt, etc. Only then can the ultimate effect be explored beyond its strict numerical characteristics. This ambitious task is to be realized through a combination of different qualitative and quantitative assessment models; scenario play – pessimistic, realistic and optimistic; cost-benefit analysis, and more.

4. Money making strategies

"Money grows on the tree of persistence."

Japanese Proverb

Once we have determined our money making character, the next step is to select our strategy. When doing so, the two main factors to consider are *time* and *risk*. With regard to the money making process, they are *in inverse relationship* – the faster we want to build wealth, the higher the risk of our strategy will be, and vice versa. This concept could be illustrated by following figure:

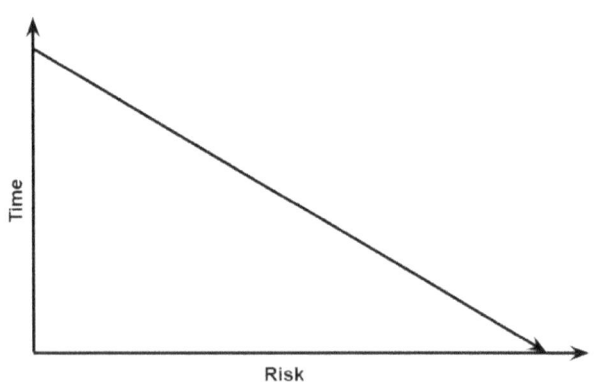

That is exactly why one cannot become rich in a blink of an eye (Let us repeat once more: winning the lottery jackpot is not a money making strategy). Again, what we are looking for is a balanced decision, i.e. the combination of time that we are ready to spend and risk that we are willing to take, in order to implement our strategy.

Although there could be many "time-risk" combinations, they may be divided into 3 main groups:

- Long term – Low risk strategy;
- Medium term – Medium risk strategy;
- Short term – High risk strategy.

Long term – Low risk strategy

Firstly, we shall look at the long term strategy. This strategy works 99.9% of the times, but it is the slowest one. This is the best strategy for everyone to start with. Below are the basic steps:

- Create our budget;
- Get debt free;
- Start to save at least 10% of our income. Anyone can do this, no matter how much they earn;

- Control our budget, with a special emphasis on the spending – do not spend money on what we do not need;
- Make sure we pay cash whenever possible, in order to limit credit card utilization;
- Invest;
- Secure our money from loss:
  - Do not invest in every idea that people propose to us;
  - Do not put all the eggs in one basket;
  - Do not trust people that are not experts.
- Plan our retirement – Most people hate to plan for their retirement. Yet it is important to protect ourselves and our family against poverty when we get older and are less able to work;
- Optional: Save money for our children's education;
- Pay out our own home early.

Ok, this is the lowest risk strategy, but the slowest one to implement. What else can be done, if we do not have the patience for it? Let us look at another strategy – more risky but with a shorter time frame:

Medium term – Medium risk strategy

- Create our budget – again we start with this very important step;
- Keep our debt, but invest the money that we would otherwise invest in reducing it.

What we mean is that we could make money, if we keep a low-interest debt, return only the minimum per month and invest the spare money. For example:

- We have a $10000 loan with interest of 1% per year;
- We have an opportunity to invest in something giving us 8% interest per year.

In this situation it is better to invest our extra money. In economic theory, this is an example of the so called interest rate differential. This is exactly what the banks do – they pay the clients low interest rate on their deposits (in return for working with their money), while at the same time they provide various credit products (using the same money) with higher interest rate. The following figure shows the interest rate differential between the loans and deposits, as it changes over time:

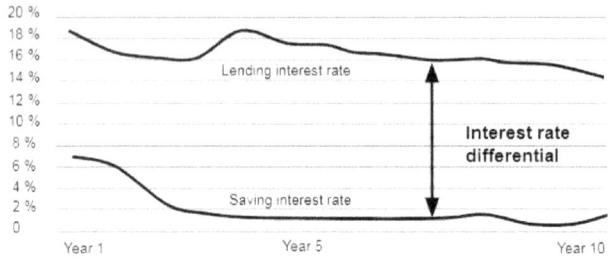

This is good strategy for medium risk people. The fact that we still owe money while investing does not reduce our stress level, but still we may be able to clear the debt quicker than with strategy 1.

Short term – High risk strategy

We highly recommend that we choose to follow a high risk strategy only after we have acquired extensive knowledge in finance. Have in mind that we discuss different strategies for money making, not some magic tricks that will make us millionaires overnight.

According to one of the basic principles in economics, there is no risk-free economic activity: the higher the risk (of losing our money), the bigger the required return from the investment. The extra money that we expect to make by taking a risk is called a risk premium.

If we are in the position of a borrower, the same logic applies – when our credit score is low, the bank considers our loan a risky one and therefore charges us with a higher interest rate (because of the higher risk premium). In other words, the bank risks here – it wants to make more money by giving a credit to someone who might not be able to pay it back.

The medium-risk strategy suggested that instead of clearing our debt, we could use the extra money to invest and make profit through the interest rate differential. The high-risk strategy takes us one step further: we borrow more money with the intention to invest it in something so profitable, that it will allow us to quickly pay back the newly-taken loan and still make extra money.

If our expectations prove wrong though, such ventures could have serious consequences on our financial health. As shown by the figure below, the negative scenario exposes us not only to losing the invested amount but to paying back the interest on top of it:

High risk takers usually invest in startups, brand new technologies, products and services. Those are really tempting and offer huge potential returns, but the big question is: how many of them will actually succeed?

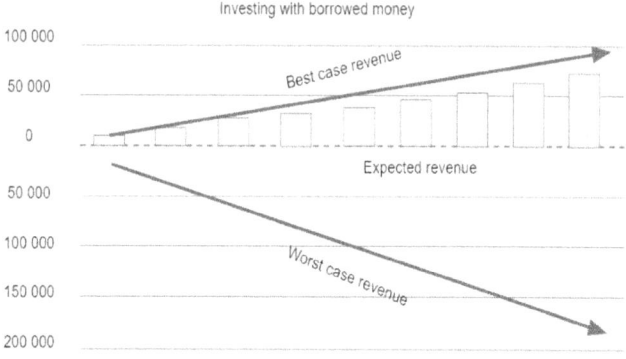

Finally, we would argue that it is a strictly individual matter, whether a certain risk is low, medium or high. Something considered very risky by one person, may be recognized as almost risk-free by another person. Along these lines, we must be aware of what our limits are, how far we can go when taking a risk.

Furthermore, as our world is changing literally by the minute, what was unthinkable a decade ago is totally mainstream today. Thus, the individual concepts of risk we talk about are constantly influenced by the general public. As a result, what one found risky some time ago, now that same person might easily find not so risky anymore. Again, it all boils down to the ability to change, adapt and build a winning mentality.

CONCLUSION

"Money is a terrible master but an excellent servant."

P.T. Barnum

Now that we already know the rules of the money-making game, let us answer the following question: "Are they very complicated and hard to follow?" We believe they are not and invite everyone who shares our opinion to join us in our journey to success. It might not be the shortest one, but if we have the courage to start it, with each step we make we will move closer to our destination – becoming wealthy.

Psychology plays a big role all along. We have learned how different the mindsets of rich and poor people are and what it takes to develop a winning personality. Bad habits, old stereotypes and excuses can give way to careful planning, determination and self-confidence.

We understood the importance and inevitability of change, went through the different phases of the change process and the emotions accompanying them. As a result, we feel better prepared for the challenges ahead.

Our next task was to get familiar with the time management basics. We found out how to use time more efficiently and effectively, reach work-life balance and avoid time wasters. Now we are convinced that we will be able to get the most of every minute.

Motivation is what makes us move forward and reach our goals. As we simply cannot afford to lose it before our mission is accomplished, we have acquired the skill to turn motivation into habit.

After that, we turned our attention to the practical aspects of money making. We went into detail about the functions of money, the structure of personal financial statements and the way interest rates work. The basic money principles served as solid foundation for our next task – to create our first budget.

Discussing the main income and expenditure items helped us realize how crucial it is to plan them in advance. In this regard, we took a close look at a number of different budget strategies, trying to find the one that best suits us. We also learned how to monitor and control our budget, in order to fulfill our long term financial goals.

In our quest to getting rich we have to overcome another major challenge - getting rid of debt. Now we are determined to do it as fast as possible, using some of the basic and supplementary debt free strategies described in the book.

Having become debt free and financially independent, we need to make our money work for us. Our newly-gained knowledge of the active and passive income sources and their specifics, the time value of money and the risk-return relationship will greatly contribute to the success of this endeavor.

The exciting world of investing, that we are about to enter, offers a multitude of money-making opportunities. We already know that our decisions should be emotionally neutral and based on thorough analysis of relevant information. Certainly, our attitude towards risk will play an important role in selecting our investment strategy.

Finally, as we have learned the rules of the money making game, we are all set to play and win it together. Game on, everyone!

ABOUT THE AUTHOR

Dr. Mariyan Genchev is an example of a person of the new age. Although he is in his mid-thirties, he has a lot of experience in store. He ceaselessly develops himself in different spheres of the social life like management and many more. He never stops looking for opportunities to learn from everything around him. His curiosity in combination with his creative abilities incite him to occupation in the field of the psychology among the rest of his interests. He finds satisfaction in helping people, in guiding others to be successful and self-confident in their lives. Due to his analytical mind and knowledge gathered during his occupation as a part time Assistant at the university, he discovers easy tricks and clever ways that can help people in our modern and entangled world to overcome the stress at work, to be successful and to be well paid for the job done. For him helping others is a mission and this book is just one of the tools helping him to complete it.

FURTHER READINGS

- Abraham Maslow, "A theory of human motivation"
- Abraham Maslow, "Motivation and Personality"
- C P Alderfer, Existence, "Relatedness and Growth: Human Needs in Organizational Settings"
- Dallas Cullen, Maslow, "Monkeys and Motivation Theory"
- Dan Ariely, "The Upside of Irrationality"
- Daniel H. Pink, "Drive: The Surprising Truth About What Motivates Us"
- Dave Ramsey, "The Total Money Makeover (Classic Edition): A Proven Plan for Financial Fitness"
- David Allen, "Getting Things Done: The Art of Stress Free Productivity"

- David Bach, "The Automatic Millionaire: A Powerful One-Step Plan to Live and Finish Rich"
- David McLelland, "The Achieving Society"
- Douglas McGregor, "The Human Side of Enterprise"
- Elisabeth Kubler-Ross, "Death and Dying"
- Elizabeth Warren, Amelia Warren Tyagi, "All Your Worth: The Ultimate Lifetime Money Plan."
- Elton Mayo, "The Human Problems of an Industrial Civilisation"
- Eric Tyson, "Personal Finance for Dummies"
- Frederick Herzberg, Bernard Mausner and Barbara Bloch Snyderman, "The Motivation to
- Gary P. Latham, "Work Motivation: History, Theory, Research and Practice"
- George S. Clason, "The Richest Man in Babylon"
- Ian Ayres, "Carrots and Sticks: Unlock the Power of Incentives to Get Things Done"
- J Kotter's "Leading Change: Why Transformation Efforts Fail
- J S Adams, "Toward an Understanding of Inequity"

- Joanne Cantor, "Mining Your Inner Moron: Why Multitasking is Such a Waste"
- John Kotter and Dan Cohen, "The Heart of Change: Real-Life Stories of How People Change Their Organizations"
- John Kotter, "Leading Change"
- L W Porter and E E Lawler, "Managerial Attitudes and Performance"
- Linda Holbeche, Understanding Change: "Theory, Implementation and Success"
- MJ DeMarco, "The Millionaire Fastlane: Crack the Code to Wealth and Live Rich for a Lifetime"
- Napoleon Hill, "Think and Grow Rich"
- Peter Drucker, "Management Challenges for the 21st Century"
- Robert Kegan and Lisa Laskow Lahey, "The Real Reason People Won't Change"
- Robert Kiyosaki, "Rich Dad Poor Dad"
- Stephen R Covey, "Seven Habits of Highly Successful People"
- Thomas J. Stanley, "The Millionaire Next Door: The Surprising Secrets of America's Wealthy"
- Tony Robbins, "MONEY Master the Game: 7 Simple Steps to Financial Freedom"
- Victor Vroom, "Work and Motivation"

www.ingramcontent.com/pod-product-compliance
Lightning Source LLC
Chambersburg PA
CBHW051305220526
45468CB00004B/1212